ON EDGAR BERGEN'S LAP

An Ironic History of the Human Condition

BILL LEVERETTE

Peachtree Publishers, Ltd.

This book is dedicated to the
first caveperson who laughed.

Published by
PEACHTREE PUBLISHERS, LTD.
494 Armour Circle, N.E.
Atlanta, Georgia 30324

Manufactured in the United States of America

1st printing

Library of Congress Catalog Number 86-63532

ISBN 0-934601-16-X

Contents

On Edgar Bergen's Lap

Prologue:
Homo obliviosus

> *It may be risky for human beings to insist too much on the criterion of self-awareness; people are fairly oblivious themselves. Socrates said that the unexamined life is not worth living. If that is true, half the world's population should be suicidal.*
> — *Time*, October 3, 1983

One beautiful morning, a busy executive gripped his steering wheel tightly as he drove hurriedly to the office. The trip from the suburbs would have been a pleasant drive if he had taken the time to enjoy it. But his mind raced ahead of the car to the office, and he was oblivious to his surroundings. He subconsciously noted the insane asylum ahead with a smattering of pity, as he did every day.

When he reached the asylum, his left rear tire blew out. He maneuvered the car to the right and pulled off on the shoulder of the road next to the asylum's chain-link fence. Muttering in anger at this disruption in his schedule, he opened the trunk and removed the jack. He hurriedly raised the car and took off the tire, but carefully placed the lug nuts in the hubcap so they wouldn't get lost.

As he rolled the flat tire around to the trunk to exchange it with the spare, a truck came speeding by close to the edge of the road. Its rear wheel slipped off on the shoulder and barely clipped the

1

edge of the hubcap. It was enough to send the hubcap sailing in the air. It landed about fifty feet away, but the lug nuts were nowhere to be found. The executive's angry muttering changed to shouted invectives as he realized he had a perfectly good spare but couldn't fasten it.

Behind the fence of the asylum, a silent man had been sitting cross-legged, watching all of this. The executive paced back and forth, waving his arms, and getting louder and more selective with his expletives. Suddenly, the man behind the fence spoke.

"Sir," he said, but the executive ignored him. "Sir!" he said again, a little louder. The executive spun around and faced him with a look of disdain that would have embarrassed a dog. The last thing he needed right now was an insane man bothering him. The inmate continued: "Sir, if you take *one* of the lug nuts off each of the other three wheels, they will hold the tire in place until you can purchase another set."

The executive was stunned. He hadn't thought of that. When he got over this shock, he began to remove the nuts from the other wheels. When he was done and the tire was mounted, he walked over to the fence and said to the inmate, "Thanks for your help. I admit I am confused, though. With a mind like yours, why are you in an insane asylum?"

The man behind the fence, still sitting cross-legged on the grass, looked up at the executive and said, "Oh, I'm *crazy*, all right, but I'm not *stupid*!"

Where is the line drawn between insanity and stupidity? A nineteenth-century zoologist, an ardent follower of Darwin's theory of evolution, tried to prove that humans evolved from the ape via *Homo stupidus*, then on to *Homo sapiens*. While descendants of the *Homo stupidus* line may occasionally be observed today, especially behind the wheel of an automobile, the creature called *Homo* has branched out into many other fields: *Homo erectus* (upright man), *Homo faber* (working, or "making," man), *Homo quaerens* (seeking man), *Homo ludens* (playing man), *Homo*

2

loquens (talking man), *Homo viator* (traveling man), *Homo religiosus* (religious man), and *Homo sapiens* (wise man). However, close examination of human history reveals that all of these are but various activities of the one true species: *Homo obliviosus* (forgetful man).

Mankind developed first in the form of *Homo erectus* since walking upright seemed to be a good way to avoid bumping into things and freed the hands for head scratching. Later came *Homo sapiens*, which meant that man had started thinking — probably about what to do next. This form rapidly developed into *Homo obliviosus*, who forgot what he was thinking about and what he had done already. (No wonder we get spells of *déjà vu*.)

There may have been no "fall" of man. Perhaps, when he thought he was ready, he jumped — although it may have been that *she* pushed him, a theory reinforced by the story of Adam and Eve. We have no other recorded admission of this possibility.

Now that sex has entered into this, a philological disclaimer is offered to the female members of the species: all references, until we get another set of words, to man, mankind, he, him, *Homo*, etc., include you, although at times you may be ashamed to admit it.

> *He looks like he just fell off Edgar Bergen's lap.*
> — David Steinberg

Anthropologists tell us that the human intellect has been in operation since prehistory in virtually the same form as we know it today. Although man's artifacts, culture, and technology have reached differing levels of sophistication throughout history, a complete human, with the same basic human nature, has been a constant since the beginning of mankind. Philosophers often discuss the constant and universal principles of human nature.

This is not to say that, at different times and in different places, people have not thought different things. They have, and they have thought them differently — even *seen* them differently. It has been said that the ancient Greeks perceived only three colors in the rainbow. Until, that is, some fellow claimed to see a fourth color. They put him away, of course, and it was not until a large number of people agreed that, by golly, there *was* a fourth color that some began to look for a fifth.

What *is* implied in the ongoing story of people is that human nature, whatever it is, never changes. Or to put it another way, once oblivious, always oblivious. And what makes people oblivious is a combination of the three basic motivations of *Homo obliviosus*: belief, knowledge, and power. Belief is the search for the reason strange things happen and Who or What causes them. Knowledge is the desire to make strange things happen regularly, and with some predictability. Power is the drive to make strange things happen, if good, to you; if bad, to someone else.

Is *obliviosus* sitting, like a dummy, on the lap of someone who is pulling strings? It often seems so. Many things happen unexpectedly despite the most careful planning and preparation. Unexpected events will occur, but what makes *obliviosus* oblivious is the fact that there is an innate hope that the strings *are* there — that someday "my ship will come in," or "I'll win the lottery," or "I'll meet Mr. or Ms. Right," or that some other externally oriented event will change life for the better. After all, if anything *does* go wrong, *obliviosus* can just say that Ol' Edgar pulled the wrong strings.

Part One
—●—
Belief

The way I see it, it doesn't matter what you believe, just so you're sincere.

— Charlie Brown

Snakes, Stars and Salvation

A young businessman took $100,000 from his company's safe and immediately lost it over one weekend in Las Vegas. He arrived home to find that his beautiful wife had left him for another man. Completely defeated, he drove until he came to a river, parked his car, and began to clamber over the bridge railing. Before he could go over the rail, he was stopped by a gnarled hand that gripped his arm. He turned and saw an ancient, exceptionally ugly woman in a black cloak. She had a wrinkled face and stringy gray hair.

"Don't jump," she rasped. "I'm a witch, and I'll grant you three wishes — for a slight consideration."

"I'm beyond help," he replied, and told her his troubles.

"Nothing to it," she cackled. "Abracadabra! The money is back in the vault. Abracadabra! Your wife is home waiting for you with love in her heart. Abracadabra! You now have a personal bank account of $200,000."

The man, struck speechless, was finally able to ask, "What . . . what is the consideration I owe you for all this?"

She smiled toothlessly. "You must spend the night with me."

The thought of staying with the old crone was the most repulsive thing he had ever experienced, but he decided it was worth it. In the morning, the distasteful ordeal was over and he was dressing to go home when the old bat propped up in bed and asked, "Say, Sonny. How old are you?"

"I'm forty-two," he replied. "Why?"

She squinted her beady eyes at him and said, "Ain't you a little old to believe in witches?"

While everyone has to believe in something, some people can believe as many as six impossible things before breakfast. In the days of *erectus,* man looked up at the stars in wonder. At first they were thought to be campfires of other tribes. Later, a few creative types began to see outlines of creatures and gods up there.

While some were looking up in awe, others were looking down in fear, for they had learned that the bite of a snake would put them to sleep for a long, long time. Having come down out of the trees to live on the ground, they returned to them at night to sleep, thinking that they would be safe from the snakes. Besides, they could see the sky-pictures better from up there.

From these beginnings, man learned the three basic elements of belief: fear of things that caused very long sleeps, one of the most common being snakes; wonder at things beyond reach or understanding, initially represented by stars; and the salvation of a refuge between the danger below and the mystery above.

– 1 –

They're Not Dead, They're Only Sleeping

Either this man is dead or my watch has stopped.
— Groucho Marx

The reverend was making one of his occasional home visits. As the family sat around the living room discussing various topics, the subject of heaven arose, as it inevitably did. The reward for living a good life was avidly discussed by the adults while little Johnny listened silently. Wishing to draw him into the conversation, the pastor looked at the boy and asked, "Johnny, would *you* like to go to heaven?" The little fellow looked back at the reverend and quickly answered, "No, thank you."

His parents were aghast, and the pastor was struck speechless. Johnny's father was the first to speak. "You mean . . . you don't want to go to *heaven*? Do you want to go . . . somewhere . . . else . . . to the *other* place?" The father couldn't bring himself to say *hell*, or even to think that his son could go there.

Johnny looked up at his father and said, "I don't want to go to *either* place."

By this time, the pastor found his tongue and, very calmly, tried to use his training in the art of gentle persuasion to convince the boy that heaven was to be desired. "Now, Johnny," he said, "heaven is a very beautiful place. You can have anything you want there. You can have ice cream or candy or whatever you want, whenever you want it. You will be happy. Now, are you *sure* you don't want to go to heaven when you die?"

Johnny quickly replied, "Oh, sure! When I die — I thought you meant you were getting up a load right now."

You don't have to be old to have an opinion about death. Fourteen-year-old Emmeline Grangerford in Mark Twain's *The Adventures of Huckleberry Finn* was obsessed with painting "mourning pictures," ladies weeping over tombs or reading a letter bearing the sad news. In her diary, she copied down the deaths and fatal accidents she read in the *Presbyterian Observer*, to which she added the poems that these misfortunes inspired in her. Huck says, "She warn't particular; she could write about anything you choose to give her to write about just so it was sadful."

That doesn't make Emmeline particularly different from anyone else who has puzzled over the meaning of death. What death is and what happens after it have occupied man's consciousness ever since he became capable of thought. The fear of death implies a desire to survive and, at the same time, inspires the conjecture of spiritual survival in an afterworld.

Every active expression of life is a denial of the final consequence of time. Will mankind ever discover the fountain of youth? Will we be able, someday, to live forever? As Samuel Goldwyn once put it, in two words: im possible. Failing that, many believers solve the mortality problem by embracing the idea of an afterlife, either as some form of paradise or as reincarnation for another life on earth, possibly even in Philadelphia.

> *Tyrawley and I have been dead these two years; but we don't choose to have it known.*
> — Lord Chesterfield

The first horn of this dilemma — the attempt at immortality — has been dealt with in many ways. One way is through preservation of the physical body. An example is given in *The Living Past*, by Ivar Lissner:

> The man who began the Great Wall of China was Ch'in Shih-huang-ti, the Emperor of China from 221-210 B.C., and a half-crazed genius who wanted to live forever. He had the magicians — the chemists of those times — working day and night to manufacture "elixirs of life," traveling far and wide for mysterious ingredients in their attempts. Apparently, the efforts were in vain, for the emperor died in 210 B.C.
>
> "But he *must not* die!" whispered the palace eunuchs and councilors. So they placed the lifeless body of their emperor in his sedan chair and carried him throughout the country, where he gave [silent] audiences from behind a curtain and, in a manner of speaking, lived on after his death.
>
> Eventually, his corpse began to give off an unpleasant smell, and huge barrels of salted fish were stacked near the emperor's sedan chair so that the smell of fish would cancel out the imperial odor. Finally — after *nine months* — even the fish would no longer do, and the emperor had to be buried.

The desire for physical immortality has not been realized by anyone unless they have an unlisted phone number and are keeping the secret to themselves. Efforts to preserve the *body*, in some manner, is common and has been done (or attempted unsuccessfully, as in the case of Ch'in) ever since they modeled clay likenesses on the skulls of the departed in Jericho, about six or eight thousand years ago.

Mummification is one of the methods of physical preservation that comes immediately to mind, although it has a history of dubious results. Egyptians were rather prolific in the manufacture of mummies once they got the hang of the process. Almost as prolific, thousands of years later, were the public unwrappings held by amateur archeologists (read: grave-plunderers) of the nineteenth century. They unwrapped — in some cases, with the help of hammer and chisel — a lot of mummies who were hoping to be left alone for eternity.

Once unwrapped, they did not go to waste, however. Many books today have pages made from the rags unwrapped from mummies. At one time, there was a large trade in these rags, and many graves were robbed and the bodies thrown aside in the gathering of raw materials for linen paper. Later, someone must have gone back for the bodies because there was also a big trade in ground-up mummies. The powder was supposed to be good for a number of things, none of which was immortality.

> *These be the dreams of baby minds.*
> — Sir Richard Burton, *The Kasidah*

While many ancient mummies suffered a dishonorable fate, some more recent ones have fared better. Jeremy Bentham furnishes an example of planned physical immortality. The founder of the philosophy of Utilitarianism (the greatest good for the greatest number) decided in 1830 to leave behind the most un-utilitarian thing he could think of. He specified in his will that his body was to be dissected, reassembled, dressed in a suit of his clothes, and seated in one of his favorite chairs so that he would be present at future meetings of his Society of Utilitarians. As Woody Allen said: "Eighty percent of success is just showing up."

Bentham had a pair of glass eyes made to fit his head, and he used to upset his friends by taking them out of his pocket at dinner and rolling them around on the table. He willed that his head was to be mummified and placed atop the clothed figure. Unfortunately, the head soon became rather grotesque and was replaced by a wax likeness.

His friends did, for a time, wheel his "reconstruction" up to the head of the table at their meetings, as he requested, but the society passed away itself, and the remains were sent to a college in London. On occasion, old Jeremy is called back into service, as in 1959 when a committee planning the publication of his works wheeled him out and had him sitting with them for publicity photos.

Another example of physical immortality, in this case unplanned, was discovered during the 1970s. In the Tunnel of Love at an amusement park in a northeastern city, the couples who sailed the dark waterway were frightened by the hanging figure of a man, its face painted red. Of course, it was all in fun. The dummy didn't *really* look like a man, after all.

One night a young man, who had apparently been through the tunnel with other paramours and knew what to expect, decided to demonstrate his bravado by playfully striking out with his hand at the dummy. He hit its arm, which, with a brittle crack, broke off. The fun ended then, for out of the shoulder protruded about eight inches of human bone.

It turned out that some unnamed and rather slight man had been embalmed or mummified somehow at some time in the past, and through some mischance of fate — or simply careless filing — became misplaced. He wound up in the amusement park, where someone who took him to be a dummy got hold of him. He was painted (he had received several coats of paint by the time the wag broke his arm off) and spent his time hanging in the Tunnel of Love.

When the dummy was discovered to be human, he was turned over to a local mortuary. The story got a lot of press at the time, but at last notice he was still propped up, standing in a corner of one of the mortuary rooms waiting to be claimed. There is no record that he ever has been. Given a choice, if one is not going to be buried, hanging around in a Tunnel of Love would probably be better than standing around in a mortuary.

> *Don't mourn for me now,*
> *Don't mourn for me never;*
> *I'm going to do nothing*
> *For ever and ever.*
>
> — The Tired Woman's Epitaph
> (Author unknown — but appreciated)

For those with more conventional ideas, the body is processed for burial. While this is an acceptable method of homage to the deceased, it has had its share of mishaps. In *The Hour of Our Death*, Philippe Ariès relates the following story:

> In 1723 there was much ado about an incident that would not have troubled the preparers of bodies in the fifteenth and sixteenth centuries. After the Duke of Orléans died, the body was opened in the usual way before embalming it and placing the heart in a box to take it to Val-de-Grace. During the evisceration, the prince's Great Dane was in the room. Before anyone could stop him, the dog pounced on the heart and ate a good quarter of it.

Other mishaps can occur on the way to the final resting place. A newspaper item reported that a man filed a ten-million-dollar suit against a mortuary for misplacing his late mother's body as it was being shipped for her funeral. The man checked with the airline the night before the flight and was assured the remains were ready for loading at the airport. Upon arrival at their destination, family members and friends were taken into a waiting room and told, "We can't find your mother." The suit said that an airline representative tried to make light of the situation by saying, "I hope your mother liked to travel."

Another newspaper item reported that a woman in Ohio won the right to sue over a funeral home's refusal to release her husband's body until a bill was paid. (Could this be what happened to the man in the Tunnel of Love? Maybe no one paid his bill, or his wife lost her case.)

Sometimes your troubles aren't over when you get there. Still another news item told of an Arizona county's plans to bury paupers two to a grave. Because of a space shortage in the potter's field, the bodies were to be stacked, one pauper's body buried eight feet deep and the other four feet deep. Two headstones would be placed side by side (an example of a modern condograve, the ancient counterpart of which will be considered later).

Sometimes, unconventional burial procedures are precipitated by unusual causes of death, as in the story of the man who worked in a carpet factory. One day, when he was not being particularly attentive, he was involved in an accident — caught up in a weaving machine. By the time his co-workers shut the thing off, he had been woven into sixteen yards of three-ply nylon carpet. Everyone who attended the funeral commented on the unusual coffin — *very* long, wide and flat. His widow said she didn't feel right about rolling him up.

When death happens suddenly, the job of announcing someone's demise is a very sensitive action, requiring a good deal of tact and sympathy, somewhat more than that demonstrated by the man who was sent to inform a woman of her husband's heart attack and death at the office: "Is the Widow Jones in?" he asked when the woman answered the door. "The *Widow* Jones?" she replied. "No, sir!" The man looked her in the eye and said, "I'll bet $10 she is!"

Billy, in one of his nice new sashes,
Fell in the fire and was burnt to ashes;
Now, although the room grows chilly,
I haven't the heart to poke poor Billy.

— Harry J.C. Graham,
Tenderheartedness

Another acceptable and somewhat neater process for disposing of the body is cremation. A company specializing in cremation advertises as follows:

- Your ashes may be scattered at sea or delivered per your instructions to a friend or relative. [See note 1.]
- You will be doing something nice for those who care about you. [See note 2.]
- Without the presence of a dead body, services may be held at a place and time most meaningful and convenient to your family and friends. [See note 3.]
- The complete charge need not be paid until time of death. [See note 4.]
- Lifetime membership: $15 ($25 for couples). [See note 5.]

Notes

1. Make a list of ten people who would appreciate receiving your ashes, and a list of five ways they could be delivered.
2. It is not clear whether this means dying or being cremated.
3. For example, Joe's Bar and Grill, during halftime of the Super Bowl game.
4. If you live alone, you will have to be rather quick to accomplish this.
5. What, no group discounts?

Reading this cremation ad almost makes you want to say "Handy-Dandy." Perhaps there will soon be ads for burial in a motor home: "When you go, you keep on going."

Coincidentally, the same newspaper that ran the cremation ad published, later the same year, an exposé about one disreputable crematorium that put everybody together in one fire, to save costs, it is supposed, and simply divided the ashes into appropriate portions for the services. It goes without saying that only a disreputable company would do such a thing, but how would you ever know? Or rather, does it really matter?

If that seems a trifle morbid, compare it with the delightful final anecdote in Joe Klein's book *Woody Guthrie, A Life*. In it, he relates the story of how Woody's wife, Marjorie, and the children, Arlo, Nora and Joady, disposed of Woody's cremated remains.

Marjorie wanted to spread the ashes from a jetty at Coney Island, a favorite spot of Woody's. The first logistical problem they faced was how to get the can opened. It was a drab olive canister that looked, according to Klein, like "an institution-size can of beans."

Marjorie located a beer-can opener and pried several holes in the top, but the ashes wouldn't pour out when they tried to distribute them from the jetty. "It's not coming," Arlo said, waving the can about. "What should I do?" No one had any ideas, so Arlo heaved the can out into the ocean. It bobbed, floated back toward the jetty, then finally sank.

Marjorie and the kids stared at the water for a while. Trying to imagine what Woody might suggest under the circumstances, Marjorie said: "Well, why don't we go to Nathan's and have a hot dog?"

> *The average man, who does not know what to do*
> *with his life, wants another one which will last forever.*
> — Anatole France

17

If the first horn of the dilemma — physical immortality — seems to be unsuccessful in varying degrees, at least the memories of the persons involved are made more vivid in proportion to the foolishness of the episodes.

The second horn of the dilemma — acceptance of the fact of mortality but with hope of eternal life in the hereafter — does not have physical manifestations that you can smell, wrap, paint, stuff, scatter to the winds or dump into the sea. What it does have in its favor is desire and belief. Similar descriptions of an afterworld have been found on five continents, and many attempts have been made to communicate with those believed to be "on the other side."

A couple of years ago, a magazine article reported on a company in California that would deliver a message of fifty words to friends and relatives long since dead. The company delivered these mystical telegrams by way of a terminally ill patient. The fee was forty dollars, of which the messenger's heirs were paid ten dollars (25 percent commission). After the money had changed hands, the messengers simply read each message. There was no need to commit it to memory since, as the company president stated, "The spirit is able to recall all things from life." At the time of the article, the company had already distributed twenty-five hundred telegrams to fifteen ailing messengers, six of whom had "recently departed." The president commented that "The greatest opposition comes from the clergy. They had a monopoly on heaven for years."

So did the mystics. Seances have been around for a long time, whereat you could "talk" directly to the departed without the messenger (or "middleman," thereby saving 25 percent if it were passed on to the consumer, which is not likely in fortune-teller economics). All calls do not get answered, however. They finally gave up on waiting for Houdini to call home.

The idea of using a "one-way" messenger is not new. None of the ideas of *obliviosus* are. Aside from sacrificial offerings, records show that the method was used at least as early as the rule of the Emperor Claudius (A.D. 41-54). Claudius was fond of playing judge and executing people, often for the slightest offense. He had a problem, however, remembering whom he had ordered slain. One day at mealtime, he asked absent-mindedly: "Why does the Empress not appear at table?" He was carefully reminded that he had previously ordered the execution of his wife, Messalina. At other times, men he had put to death were summoned to appear before him. When they didn't show up, he executed messengers to tell them they were incurable dullards.

> *I do not believe in an afterlife, although I am bringing a change of underwear.*
> — Woody Allen

An important part of belief in the hereafter is packing the bags for the trip. There have always been people who thought you couldn't get into heaven unless you brought a covered dish.

In lower Egypt, long ago, people buried their dead in "grave-dwellings" above the ground and shared their daily meals with them. In the voodoo cults of the last two centuries, meals were placed on the graves with a ring of coins around the perimeter of the plate to ward off *gris-gris* — bad luck, or a curse. Of course, the plates were empty and the coins gone by morning, so they knew the offerings were accepted, and encouraged by a group of living, smiling freeloaders.

Everyone is familiar with the tombs of the Pharaohs, with their riches and utensils to make life a little easier in the hereafter. The freeloaders also got to those, beginning soon after the tombs were closed. But the Egyptians were not the only ones who prepared elaborate luggage for the trip to glory. The practice is spread throughout history.

The Russian archaeologist Weselowski dug up an extremely interesting Scythian burial mound. In the lower chamber lay the dead chieftain, and above him were buried the thirteen or more people who accompanied him into death. Around the rectangle of the grave were found skeletons of twenty-two horses. This is tantamount to someone being buried today with all friends and co-workers, both family automobiles, the TV set, and anything else the bank doesn't carry off before the funeral.

Did the "thirteen or more" people buried with the chieftain go willingly? It seems so, possibly under the influence of something. In a number of burial sites, each person had a goblet of some type in hand or nearby.

> *I don't know what she was in her previous life, but I notice she always turns around three times before lying down.* — BL

The attempt to thwart mortality by believing in an afterlife has another aspect. It was called metempsychosis by Pythagoras and his ilk; now it is called reincarnation. The hereafter, to these believers, is simply *here* after. Job cried out, "If a man die, shall he live again?" Many seem to think so, especially those who are not having a great time in this life. "Oh, well," they say, "this one doesn't count. Wait till next time!"

A lot of famous people believe (or *have* believed or *will* believe) in reincarnation. There is no point in naming them. Just because they were/are famous in one incarnation doesn't mean that they weren't/aren't slobs or triflers in another. For the skeptic who refuses to give much credence to the opinions and beliefs of others, it is best to rely solely on scientific fact. Anyone who doubts the validity of reincarnation has never observed employees coming back to life at quitting time.

It would seem, from all of the previous examples, that attempts at physical immortality have been met with questionable success, if not abject failure. As for spiritual immortality, all we have are our own individual beliefs. Despite the books written about near-death experiences, we have not "heard" from anyone about what to expect — should we pack a sweater?

Our pagan ancestors were taught to believe in a barren, cold, homeless hell in the far north. When the Christian missionaries appeared, they were delighted by their description of hell as an enormous bonfire. "At least we will keep warm," they cried joyfully.

The hereafter, if there is one other than here, may be a land of milk-and-honey or a city of streets paved with gold or simply a bright light. And if it is any of these, no wonder the departed are not heard from. Why would they bother? *They're* not worrying about dying, and they would have no sense of urgency to communicate with someone who will show up sooner or later, anyway.

* * *

Famous Last Words:

I always talk better lying down.
— James Madison

Don't let it end like this. Tell them I said something.
— Pancho Villa

Why, they couldn't hit an elephant at this dist . . .
— General Sedgwick

I don't see how they make a profit out of this stuff at a dollar and a quarter a fifth.
— Anonymous Sot

21

– 2 –

Fate Strikes Again!
Sheep's Liver at Ten

Due to unforeseen circumstances, the Psychic Convention will not be held.

— Las Vegas newspaper

While driving across Manhattan, a man hears a small, ghostly voice saying, "Go to Las Vegas! Go to Las Vegas!" On an impulse, he turns the car around and heads west. Four days later he's rolling into Las Vegas when the same voice says, "Go to the Lucky Club! Go to the Lucky Club!" So he drives to the Lucky Club and walks into the casino. The little voice is more excited now: "Go to table three! Go to table three!" And he goes to table three. The voice is beside itself: "Bet a thousand dollars on 26! Bet a thousand dollars on 26!" Caught up in the spirit of the thing, the man whips out his wallet, pulls out a thousand dollars and throws it on number 26. The wheel spins, the ball bounces from number to number, then finally — with a sickening clunk — drops into number 13.

The man becomes hysterical and yells, "Voice! You told me to come to Las Vegas, to go to the Lucky Club, to go to table three, to bet a thousand dollars on number 26! I did everything you said and I lost. I lost a thousand dollars!" And the voice answered, "How about that! How about that!"

Throughout the ages, *obliviosus* has followed, lemming-like, anyone who seemed to have the ability to foretell the future. There has never been a shortage of oracles, shamans, magicians, priests and astrologers to see signs and portents in the lumps of sheep's livers and the configuration of stars, or to serve as intermediaries between the "voice" of whatever god they represented and anyone who would listen. Always mysterious, usually equivocal, occasionally correct, these "voices," from the diviners of Babylon to the astrological columns in today's newspapers, have enticed man with their promise.

Although *obliviosus* may have forgotten a lot of his history, he still wants to know what's happening — next. In the weekend newspapers, there are two horoscope columns, one to tell you what the stars have planned for you on Sunday and one to tell you what they have planned for Monday. It is not clear whether this is a device to give the astrological diviners a day off or to give the readers a chance to decide if next week is worth entering. In *The Living Past*, Ivar Lissner says: "All the thoughts, actions of the Sumerians were focused upon the future. The prophet-priests of the Sumerians, the *baru*, knew everything. They controlled the lives of their people for three thousand years. Generation after generation they compared the course of events with the condition and appearance of sheep's livers."

A belief that controls people's lives for three thousand years is no passing fancy. Assuming that everyone knows what the lumps and markings on a sheep's liver look like, the perspective of time relative to this particular belief begs a little reflection.

Three thousand years, at twenty-five years per generation, translates into 120 generations. Fourteen generations ago, Shakespeare was looking for ideas to write another play. Forty generations ago, we were in the Dark Ages. One hundred generations ago, Socrates was teaching Plato a few things about thinking. One hundred twenty generations ago (three thousand years), takes us back to the Phoenicians, who were replacing inconvenient clay tablets with ink, paper, and their new invention, the alphabet.

A lot can happen in 120 generations. It would seem that on the scale of total recorded history, sheep's livers went out about the time reading and writing came in. Of course, the divination of the future by observing the lumps and markings on sheep's livers seems absurd to most civilized people today. It was, however, believed in by millions of people for thousands of years. The millions of far more civilized people who live today know better than to believe such foolishness:

Horoscope For Tomorrow

VIRGO (Aug. 23—Sept. 22): If you can read this, today could be your day. Circumstances take sudden turn in your favor — you'll be at right place at crucial moment. Exude confidence, wear bright colors. Stay away from all other signs of the zodiac. Food plays a key role.

— Newspaper feature

Tonight's Forecast: Dark
— BL

While the methods of divination may have changed, the interpreters of the signs and portents — oracles, shamans, magicians — have always been among *obliviosus*, ready to step forward to answer the question "Why?" Even in the paleolithic caves (five hundred generations ago, to use the same scale of time), someone was ready to slip into an animal skin, jump out of a dark corner, and scare the heck out of everybody. While the shaman didn't answer the question "Why?" a lot of people were too nervous to ask it again.

Throughout Eastern and Western literature, there are references that equate "blind" with "stupid" and "madmen" with "prophets." *When madmen lead the blind . . . in the country of the blind, the one-eyed man is king . . .* speaking in parables because "they seeing see not, and hearing they hear not, neither do they understand." The children in T. S. Eliot's trees are not seen. The chained people in Plato's allegory of the cave are unseeing by choice. Blind is equated with "not seeing" — possibly "not looking " — and madmen are visionaries who see something that is there, which no one wants to look at, and are condemned for pointing it out.

The Greek story-telling historian, Herodotus, reported that when the Scythian king fell sick, he sent for the three soothsayers of the most renown at the time. They spread their willow rods on the ground and uttered prophecies. Usually they blamed the king's illness on someone not present who had sworn against the king. At the time, according to Herodotus, everyone swore against the king, but nobody got caught at it until the king got sick.

The man accused by the soothsayers was arrested and brought before the king. The soothsayers told him that, according to their art, he was guilty. The accused told them that they were liars, denied the charge, told them what they could do with their art, and complained of the injustice to the king.

The king made no decision. Instead, he sent for six new soothsayers and got a second opinion. If they agreed with the first three accusers, the man was found guilty and beheaded by the original three, who then divided his goods among themselves.

If, however, the six consultants acquitted the man, other soothsayers, and more, and more were sent for to try the case until, it is supposed, the king was satisfied that the first three had made a mistake. If most decided in favor of the man's innocence, the first three soothsayers were bound and gagged, thrown into a wagon filled with brushwood, a fire was set to the brushwood, and the oxen — rather rapidly — departed with the false prophets.

> *Worth seeing? Yes; but not worth going to see.*
> — Samuel Johnson

Those who scoff at fortune tellers and soothsayers will pay money to see a magic show. As far back as the Magdalenian era (14,000-9,000 B.C.) — for example, at Lascaux, France — beautiful yet mysterious images were painted and sculpted in dark caverns hidden deep in the earth.

Scholars are divided in their explanations of these representations. Some say they were simply an outlet of the artistic impulse for its own sake; others see in them a magical purpose. The second explanation is the more probable because it is more analogous to the practices of primitive people today. The caves may have been sacred places, either to insure success in the hunt or, if the images came after the herds had departed, to lament the passing of a time of plenty and to attempt, through ritual, to make it return.

But it did not return, for them. Something else happened. In *The History of Man*, Gustav Schenk gives one opinion:

> *Homo magus* [man the magician], the transcendent man, turned into a *Homo faber* [man the maker]. The gods and spirits abandoned him; he must trade if he wished to survive. The cold overpowering of nature began and therewith the separation from her. Divinatory powers declined; inspiration, intuition and the approach from within were replaced by a will that, spurred on by the imagination and the understanding

which had been awakened, appropriated everything with determined tenacity and deliberately created a new material reality. The magic enchantment had been broken and the vision was lost. Did magical man, with his creative artistic power, come to an end everywhere and at the same time? Did then the discovery of the plough some 9000 years ago plough up the ancient soul layer of *Homo magus*?

For most, maybe. Yet some among *Homo* managed to retain the ability to perform magic. Sheep's livers aside, we find examples far back in recorded history. When Moses threw down his rod, it became a serpent. His brother Aaron learned how to do this, and they went to the Pharaoh to show him the trick. The Pharaoh must have seen it before because he retaliated by having his magicians — the wise men and sorcerers — throw down *their* rods and they became serpents also. Neither serpents nor magic were strangers to the Egyptians. Then, in one of the earliest recorded examples of one-upmanship, Aaron's rod/serpent swallowed up all the other rod/serpents.

> *I always keep a supply of stimulant handy in case I see a snake — which I also keep handy.*
> — W. C. Fields

Most magicians, oracles and shamans use attention-getting devices or training aids in the performance of their acts. Snakes have been familiars since the beginning of time — at least, what *obliviosus* considers the beginning: the creation mythology that abounds throughout the world. The subtle rascal that was reported to have tempted Eve in Eden was a serpent of the persuasive variety, as opposed to the fire-breathing, flying, squeezing or decorative kinds which came later.

The snake has been represented in many, if not all, cultures. On Roman coins, in the statuettes of Crete, at the temple of Babylon . . . so much so that it makes one wonder how this creature slithered its way into the imagination of so many people.

In Polynesia, from Hawaii to New Zealand to Easter Island where there are no snakes, they have adopted the monster eel — called *Te Tuna* — which serves the same purpose. In Ireland, where they have no snakes either, they have a story about Saint Patrick running them out of the country, so it seems that they once had them.

In antiquity, the snake represented the renewal of life because its home was in the earth and it annually shed its skin. But we live in a scientific age when the only thing that resembles a fire-breathing serpent is a heat-seeking missile on its way to a target and the only messages about the renewal of life come to *obliviosus* via the pulpits, live or through the magic of television.

There are, however, those who still use snakes in magical ceremonies. Cults of snake worshipers exist, usually in rural or primitive areas. Just a few years ago, a newspaper reported:

> Bangkok, Thailand — Hundreds of villagers are flocking to a thatched hut to fork out $1.30 and pay homage to a holy albino cobra that sips tea and sleeps in front of an electric fan. The sacred snake was captured last week [by a villager] who immediately carried it to a local spiritualist. The medium pronounced the four and a half-foot-long reptile sacred, and [the villager] has amassed a small fortune charging fellow villagers as much as $1.30 each to pay homage to the snake. It has attracted a steady stream of worshipers and a substantial income.

There are three notable features of this item: first, while the snake benefited as much as the villager in this arrangement, it should be noted that at no time did the snake itself profess to be sacred — it was the medium who said it was; second, if there is any magic at all in this, it is that the villager got away with it; and third, it would seem, for all those who paid $1.30, that self-deception is better than no belief at all.

> *Anyone who doesn't believe in fate has never run out of toilet paper, Kleenex, napkins and paper towels at the same time.*
>
> — BL

"Something the matter?" asked the girl of her young, well-dressed male friend.

"Two months ago my grandfather died and left me eighty-five thousand dollars," said the young man.

"That doesn't sound like anything to be upset about," the girl replied. "It should happen to me."

"Yeah," he grumbled, "but last month an uncle on my mother's side passed away. He left me $150,000."

"So why are you sitting there looking so unhappy?"

"This month, so far, not a cent."

Some naturally gifted, reasonable people strive to succeed, yet fail. Others, without visible redeeming qualities, succeed, often in spite of themselves. Is it fate, chance, providence, luck, fortune — or is it "just one of those things"?

Neoplatonism, a school of philosophy founded at Alexandria in the third century A.D., attributed providence to divine will, fate to the law which rules all things according to their nature, fortune to the power which decides between constancy and the rare or unusual occurrence, and chance to accidents which negate the possibility of predicting an outcome.

Aristotle claimed that luck is connected with nature rather than a deity. The lucky man is defined as one who "has an impulse without reason toward goals which he actually sets, and such an impulse is natural." Which is to say that, by nature, we are impelled toward things for which we are well-fitted, hence, "lucky."

If you wait too long for your ship to come in, you may be too tired to unload it.

— BL

The question of free will arises occasionally in the mind of *obliviosus*. Can humans not determine, by using free will, the outcome of a life or an endeavor? There are many forks in the road of life, and people have a choice at each one. Some choices are influenced by something ahead on one of the roads, some by something on the road behind; one enticing, the other impelling the traveler in a certain direction. Occasionally, when there is time to stand at the fork and contemplate the options, a conscious, willful choice may be possible. It may also happen that, while standing at the fork in contemplation, a rock may fall on the traveler's head.

If the pausing to contemplate is considered a choice in itself, along with the many roads going in many directions, then there is initial freedom of choice at each moment in human conduct. But once a choice is made, fate comes into control. Events are fateful only *after* the exercise of free will. Until the next fork. Except for accidents.

All this is made somewhat clearer in mythology. The three Fates — Clotho, Lachesis and Atropos — govern the laws of events. Fortune is a deity who enters the celestial senate and proceeds to shock everyone with her unexpected behavior. Everyone knows someone like that. She interferes with the Fates by introducing unforeseen and sudden outbursts. Not satisfied with being in control of accidents, she claims to control cause and effect as well. When she does that, she is associated with Nemesis, the goddess of retribution. (Providence will appear later, when we discuss manifest destiny.)

> *Fate leads the willing, drags the unwilling.*
> — Cleanthes

History's fateful moments seem to have been touched by the unexpected behavior of Fortune. When, in 1920, King Alexander of Greece died from a bite by his pet monkey, the accident started a series of events which led Sir Winston Churchill to remark that "a quarter of a million persons died of this monkey's bite."

Other examples abound: if Cleopatra or Helen had been ugly; if Trotsky had not gone duck hunting; if Columbus's ships had gone over the edge. But these are big-time, world-shaking, momentous examples. What about the average *obliviosus*? In the following examples, try to match the events to one of the following causes:

    a.) Fate
    b.) Providence
    c.) Chance
    d.) Fortune
    e.) Nemesis
    f.) Murphy's Law.

(If you get any right, you're lucky.)

Sure, Hindsight Is Easy

A couple is casually conversing while leaning against a lifeboat on an ocean liner. In a while, they stroll away arm in arm, allowing us to see the printed inscription on the lifeboat: "TITANIC"!

— Newspaper movie review

Crossed The Street Just In Time

A great white shark blocked traffic on a North Hollywood street for about an hour. A 3,200-pound replica of a shark's head crashed to the pavement as workers switched billboard movie ads, swapping *Jaws 3-D* for *Scarface*. The only thing the shark bit was the pavement.

— Newspaper item

Defective Zippers Can Be Hazardous To Your Health

An Arkansas man was killed when he rolled off a railroad flatcar in his sleeping bag and fell 120 feet to his death. The Sheriff's department said the incident happened Thursday night as a train was crossing a bridge over the Feather River Canyon. A friend traveling with the victim crawled along twenty-four cars to notify the engineer, who stopped at the first chance and notifed the Sheriff's office. Deputies found the sleeping bag hooked to the Rock Creek Bridge and the man's body on the rocks 120 feet below.

— Newspaper item from wire reports

Better Look Elsewhere For A Reference

An eight-year-old boy died of a heart attack when his two hundred-pound babysitter slipped and fell on top of him. It was ruled an accidental death.

— Newspaper item

The Russians Will Now Claim They Invented Murphy's Law

Venera 14, a Russian spacecraft that, along with its sister ship, 13, touched down on Venus in a mission to sample Venusian soil and measure its density. To film the event, Venera 14 had a camera that was protected by a special lens cap programmed to pop off during the landing. It popped off, the mechanical arm with a spring-loaded plunger reached out for its one chance to sample the Venusian soil, and landed directly on top of the lens cap.

— Magazine item

* * *

Victims of accidents sometimes willingly invoke Nemesis, the goddess of retribution, known to children as revenge.

While innocently playing in the house, a little girl accidentally knocked over her mother's favorite antique vase, shattering it to pieces. The mother was so irate she shut the child in a big, dark closet to punish her.

For fifteen long minutes the door was closed without a sound from behind it. At last the anxiety overcame the anger, and the mother opened the door. Peering into the darkness, she could see nothing.

"What are you doing in there?" she questioned.

Slowly and with emphasis, a small voice replied: "I'm thpitin' on your new hat, and thpitin' on your new dress, and I'm thpitin' in your new thatin thlippers, and . . . and . . .

There was a breathless pause.

"And what are you doing now?" the mother asked nervously.

"Waiting for more thpit!" said the voice of vengeance.

— 3 —
Gimme Dat
Ol' Time Religun

*If God lived on Earth, people would break His
windows.*

— Jewish Proverb

The glass of the goldfish bowl was uneven, giving the sunlight that struck it a prismatic effect. Rays of many-colored light bounced off the gravel at the bottom, lending a mystical quality to the water.

One of the goldfish, feeling particularly mystical itself, swam over to another goldfish and bubbled out a question: "Do you think there really is a God?"

The other goldfish opened and closed its mouth several times, let out a large bubble, then replied: "Why, of course! Who do you think changes the water every day?"

The first God was a mother. If belief began with the fear of death, the miracle of birth gave *obliviosus* something to believe in. Sculptures from the early and late Stone Age depict fertile females, the evident forerunners of the named goddesses Gaea, Rhea, Cybelle, Axeiros, Potnia, Innana, Ishtar, Astarte, Isis, Aphrodite or Venus, Ma or Ammas, Matera Teija — all of which are appellations indicating Mother of the Gods, Great Mother, Divine Mother or, as we would say today with a greatly diminished understanding, Mother Earth or Mother Nature.

In prehistory, the Great Goddess was thought to be the source of life. Many of the goddesses combined the roles of virgin and mother and were often associated with a young male god who was not immortal by nature, but had died and been raised to life again. Some of the early "dying-rising" gods were Mithra, Tammuz, Attis, Adonis and Osiris.

Mankind's notion of gods and goddesses evolved as the world evolved. In Egypt, at one time, every village had its own special gods or goddesses. Some were animals, some mere objects, and some were personified forces of nature.

About four thousand years ago, a man named Pharaoh Akhenaten decided that it would be somewhat more appropriate, not to say more organized, to worship a single universal God — in this case, represented by the sun. Everyone in Egypt humored him, at least publicly, but as soon as he died, they reverted to the "hometown" gods. Later, the Hebrews tried again with their idea of monotheism, one God, invisible, incorporeal, the creator of the universe. Their idea, so far, more or less, has stuck.

The problem with one God, however, is that it raises the question of whose God? Down through the centuries, the idea of God gradually departed the mind of the masses, remaining only in the viscera as faith. Among the philosophers and theologians, God became the subject of debate. Debate became argument, argument became invective, invective came to blows, and religious warfare was born. Kenneth John Macksey, in *The History of Land Warfare*, gives an example of debate gone berserk:

> The most bestial wars are those with a religious bias, and religious wars were on the increase in the fifteenth century. At the siege of Carolstein in 1422, to give an example of bacteriological attack, the bodies of the slain, along with 2000 cartloads of manure, were cata-

pulted into the city. Prior to the seige of Constantino-
ple in 1453, sulphur fumes were employed by the
Turks to gas Byzantine defenders (an example of not
only bacteriological, but chemical and psychological
warfare as well.)

It is difficult, and becomes more so as time passes, to distinguish between true religious warfare and merely ideological
warfare. Despite glamorized accounts, the crusaders were not all
religiously motivated. Many, if not most, of them got into it for
whatever spoils they could claim, especially land and gold, the
other main reasons for warfare.

The motives for some religious battles are difficult to classify.
The bloodiest civil war in history was the Great Peace Rebellion
in China (1850-1864), in which the Ming Dynasty fought the
Manchu government. The rebellion was led by Hung Hsiu-
ch'uan, who was evidently deranged. He imagined himself to be
a younger brother of Jesus Christ. He called his troops the
Heavenly Kingdom of Great Peace. Best estimates put the total
loss of life during the rebellion at between twenty and thirty
million people. You know what they say: "Peace is Hell." By
contrast, and going on at about the same time in history, slightly
less than a half-million people from both sides died in the Civil
War of the United States.

*I have already given two cousins to the war, and I
stand ready to sacrifice my wife's brother.*
— Artemus Ward

War is not the only means of human sacrifice. According to
B. F. Skinner, the behavioral scientist, governments and religions
have always used operant conditioning to get people to die for
them. Sacrifice seems to have been a standard feature of ritu-

alistic belief. All sacrificial victims died natural deaths. Any living thing that is thrown a hundred feet down a well, burned or buried alive, or has its heart torn out will naturally die.

Sacrificial victims were not limited to the beautiful maidens and captive warrior youths that the Mayans used to throw in a deep well when things weren't going right. Animals also played a big part in appeasing the gods, including the camel sacrifices of the Arabians around the fifth century B.C. But human sacrifice, in whatever form, has always had a special meaning for believers.

Some sacrificial offerings, although painful, were not fatal. From the paleolithic cavemen to the American Indians, there is evidence of chopping off finger joints in sacrifice to the gods. In *The Masks of God: Primitive Mythology*, Joseph Campbell includes the following Crow Indian prayer: "I give you this joint [of my finger], give me something good in exchange. I am poor, give me a good horse. I want to strike one of the enemy and I want to marry a good-natured woman. I want a tent of my own to live in."

Two human hands, except for someone like Anne Bolyn, who had six fingers on one hand, have a total of twenty-eight joints. If the Indian who uttered that prayer could get a horse, a good-natured woman and a tent — not to mention a coup — for one joint out of twenty-eight, it doesn't seem too bad a deal. But, at today's prices, if he wanted a pickup truck, he wouldn't be able to hold the pen to sign the papers.

Sacrifice is a forestalling or sating of time in order to benefit the one who offers the sacrifice. Many times children, usually the firstborn, were the preferred offering. The Hindu Kali is the personification of all-consuming time. Cronus was Father Time to the Greeks and later to the Romans as Saturn, after he was kicked out of Greece and emigrated to Italy.

According to legend, Cronus was to be dethroned by a son destined to be greater than he. To avoid this fate, Cronus swallowed all of his children at birth. Legend also speaks of cannibalistic mothers, who have come down to us in the form of fairy tales: the witch who lives in a candy house lures the children so she can eat them.

Heaven will protect the working girl.
— Edgar Smith

All innocent youths and virgins were not put to death. Some were sacrificed in other ways. In the Inca civilization, royal officials visited each village and classified girls who had reached the age of ten. Girls of striking beauty were taken away and put under the care and teaching of the government. The rest had to stay home and marry taxpayers.

The pretty ones were put into state schools where they learned to spin, weave, cook, and perform other domestic duties. When they finished school, some were sent to serve in the Sun temples as "Virgins of the Sun," an honor that meant they were to remain in perpetual chastity. Others were given as wives to deserving noblemen and warriors. Still others were assigned jobs as royal concubines who also had to cook the king's meals and make his clothes.

It is hard to tell whether the Inca Virgins had it better or worse than the Vestal Virgins of Roman mythology. Vesta was the goddess of the domestic hearth, and her priestesses, the Vestal Virgins, had the job of keeping the home fires burning. The girls served thirty years: ten learning their job, ten doing it, and ten teaching it to the next shift.

At the end of their service, they were allowed to remove their religious robes and return to civilian life. If they wished, they were free to marry at this time. It is hard to believe that there were many Roman men standing in line waiting to marry women with forty to fifty years of experience in being virgins.

> *The great god Ra whose shrine once covered acres*
> *is filler now for crossword puzzle makers.*
> — Keith Preston,
> *The Destiny That Shapes Our Ends*

A big feature of religion is height. Ever since the Tower of Babel, and probably before, *obliviosus* has built towers, pyramids, ziggurats, temples, churches, lighthouses, skyscrapers . . . apparently attempting to reach the heavens. Although each of these structures serves a different purpose, all are, in some way, a monumental statement that *obliviosus* wants to leave behind.

The pyramids began as pit-graves dug in desert gravel, covered with sand, and surrounded by a circle of desert stones. The size of the pits grew, then they were lined with brick; next roofs of wood, brick, and finally masonry were added. The first terraced pyramid known to us is that of King Zoser, c. 2900 B.C. It was a series of tombs, one atop another, progressively decreasing in size to form the tapered building we now know as the pyramid. So a pyramid is mainly a tomb, and Zoser's was the first condo grave in recorded history.

The word *ziggurat* comes from the Babylonian word meaning pinnacle or mountaintop. A ziggurat is solid and serves mainly to support a "high temple" at the top where a god could rest while on the way down to visit a "low temple" at ground level. The ziggurats were public shrines to which thousands marched in procession to honor their god. According to Herodotus, the Babylonian tower had at its top a temple that contained only a couch and a golden table. There were no statues of any kind, but at night a chosen woman came to keep the lonely visiting god company. It is supposed that she knew how to cook and make clothes, but Herodotus does not mention a stove or a sewing kit.

Temples are buildings devoted to a special or exalted purpose, generally the worship of a deity, and here we run into an ambigu-

ity due to mankind's various understandings of worship throughout history. For example, in Aztec temples people practiced
human sacrifice. When Cortés (or Cortez) entered the temple in
Moctezuma's (or Montezuma's) capital city, he found the image
of the god Huitzilopochtli (or Uichilobos, or Mxyztplx), who
looked like the devil to his Spanish eyes. The walls of the room
were plastered with dried human blood. Nearby, he found the
skulls of about 136,000 victims. But, incongruously, the same
temples had been used by the Mayans as observatories to develop
their calendar, which was about twenty seconds closer to sidereal
time than our Gregorian calendar and less than six seconds off the
actual sidereal reckoning. It seems that while these people were
strong on misanthropy, they didn't miss at astronomy.

Other examples, such as the Angkor Wat temple, for instance,
are places of homage — prayers in stone. Of course, some of the
temples were adjacent to the pyramids, some of the towers were
tombs, and many churches — which derived from combinations
of the above — had and have elements of temples, towers, tombs,
sacrificial (albeit symbolic) altars, statues, steps, terraces, etc.

Soldiers, forty centuries look down upon you.
— Attributed to Napoleon I before
the Battle of the Pyramids

Gentlemen, forty minutes look up at you.
— Attributed to an early pyramid builder

Before we leave the subject of monuments and memorials, it is
worth recalling the story of an early pyramid builder and the
unique way she financed her memorial, as related by Herodotus
(from a translation by George Rawlinson):

The wickedness of Cheops (Khufu) reached to such

a pitch that, when he had spent all his treasures and wanted more, he sent his daughter to the stews [the bath houses of that day, which were used as brothels] with orders to procure him a certain sum — how much I cannot say, for I was not told; she procured, however, and at the same time, bent on leaving a monument which should perpetuate her own memory, she required each man to make her a present of a stone towards the work which she contemplated. With these stones, she built the pyramid which stands midmost of the three that are in front of the great pyramid, measuring along each side 150 feet.

Will Cuppy, in *The Decline and Fall of Practically Everybody*, says that scholars figured the dimensions of the pyramid of Cheops's daughter and decided that what Herodotus said she did couldn't be done. Cuppy also says that scholars don't know about those kinds of things.

It is thought that the daughter in question may have been Hetepheres II because she had blond hair like her mother. The *Cambridge Ancient History* thinks it may have been a wig. Cuppy says she may have been the daughter of a foreigner since all Egyptians were brunettes. At any rate, there seems to have been an Aryan in the woodpile.

What are you supposed to do, rent them a motel room?
— Comment on a city ordinance forbidding animals to
engage in sex in public view

Sex has always been a tool of temptation. Everyone gets a chance to sin. Some take it. The epitome of temptation is the idea of Satan, who is also known by a lot of other names, all well-suited to his devilish personality. Satan represents darkness, the independent principle of evil, the primordial source of suffering and death, and rascality in general.

His job — and we usually think of him as a man — it's only fair — is to seduce *obliviosus*. One of the ways he does this is by using other devils and fallen angels to tempt those who apparently need tempting.

One type of evil spirit was the incubus, who lusted after the wives of men and voluntarily descended to copulate with them. And if the husband believed that, the wife could sell him a bridge in the bargain.

The clergy has always sought out, and usually found, most of these rascals. For example, between 1450 and 1750 A.D., an estimated 200,000 witches were executed in Europe and America. Recently, the charismatic movement has revived the ancient practice of casting out demons. A theological seminary in California has added a course to help future pastors distinguish between mental illness and demonic possession.

A country evangelist was in the habit of building up spectacular endings for his revival meetings. Coming to the church one Sunday, he arranged for his stunning finale by hiding a small farm boy with a caged white dove in the rafters of the ceiling.

At the appropriate moment, the parson was to shout for the Holy Ghost to come down, whereupon the dove was to be released to fly about above the congregation. The moment came, and devoutly the preacher called out, "Holy Ghost, come down!"

Nothing happened. Again he raised his voice and arms heavenward, shouting, "Holy Ghost, come down!" Nothing happened, but, after a few moments of expectant silence, the country boy poked his head out from behind the rafters and yelled: "A yaller cat done et the Holy Ghost. I gone throw down de yaller cat."

Part Two
—•—
Knowledge

So much has already been written about everything that you can't find out anything about it.
— James Thurber

Caves, Camshafts
and Consciousness

On a clear morning, three men stood at a lookout point on the south rim of the Grand Canyon and stared out at the vast panorama. One of the men was an archeologist, one a clergyman, and one a cowboy.

The archeologist said: "What a wonder of science!"

The clergyman said: "One of the glories of God!"

The cowboy said: "A heck of a place to lose a cow!"

There is no such thing as universal knowledge as long as people view the same things in different ways. Most people see what they need to see. When *obliviosus* was living in caves, if he didn't see something he needed, he invented it. He made hammers, saws, knives, needles and thread.

A while later, a few of the same creative types who had watched the star-pictures got together and made a big stone wheel. They made another, and another — and watched each of them roll thundering down the hill, out of control. They were asked to stop by an angry group wielding hammers, saws, knives and needles after one of the wheels decimated a party of hunters. The brake was not invented until thousands of years later.

While tools became available as needed, man had no machines until much later, probably after he invented labor unions. Francis Bacon, in his *Novum Organum,* pointed out that "we should notice the force, effect, and consequences of inventions, which are nowhere more conspicuous than in those three which were unknown to the ancients; namely, printing, gunpowder, and the compass. For these three have changed the appearance and state of the whole world: first in literature, then in warfare, and lastly in navigation."

But that was over three hundred years ago, and today the big three inventions that are "nowhere more conspicuous" are television, nuclear weapons, and the computer. Knowledge has brought the world instantaneous and universal dissemination of information, the ability for total destruction on an instantaneous and universal scale, and the perhaps evolutionary means of transferring the consciousness of *obliviosus* directly into a multitude of computers in the hope that *they* will know what to do next.

– 4 –

They're Putting a Highway Through the Campfire

Our national flower is the concrete cloverleaf.
—Lewis Mumford

A real-estate agent asked a woman if she wanted to buy a home.

The woman said, "A home? What do I need a home for? I was born in a hospital, educated in a college, courted in an automobile, and married in a church. I eat breakfast in a convenience store, lunch at the office out of a paper bag, and dinner in a restaurant. On the weekends, I spend mornings at the golf course, afternoons shopping, and evenings at the movies. A home? I don't need a home, I need a garage!"

Someone once said that butter came from grass. All you add is a cow and a churn. The automobile was born from the seed of grain, with a millions-of-miles long umbilical cord called road.

When *obliviosus* learned that he could remove the seeds of grain from the uplands where they grew naturally and replace them in the valleys where he wanted them to grow, agriculture began. No more hunting for food — just sitting there and watching it grow. Many people sitting around watching it grow in the same place made a village.

Sir Leonard Woolley, the English archeologist, said a village was based mainly upon agriculture, and some of its inhabitants were not food-producers, but craftsmen. Woolley said there is no clear-cut distinction between a village and a town, except that the town is larger in size, population and social organization. (One man commented that he must have come from a place smaller than a village. It was so small they had a mirror at one end. The one-room schoolhouse had planned to offer driver's education, but the mule died.

Cities begin to get a little more complicated, implying, according to Woolley, a cathedral, a clerical organization and a large number of laymen who are neither farmers, fishers nor hunters. It further implies a recognized form of municipal government and a substantial population of professional rulers, officials, clergy, artisans and merchants who do not grow or catch their own food, but who live instead on the surplus provided by others who live in towns or villages outside the city.

Jacquetta Hawkes says in *The World of the Past* that while early hunters used unobtrusive pathways, sizeable villages had well-marked tracks — ruts made from dragging sleds. The villages also had alleys, paths, lanes and streets. Roads outside of settlements, she suggests, probably did not surface before the use of wheeled vehicles.

Foodstuffs and other stuffs had to be moved to the city to feed the politicians, clergy and "laymen who were neither farmers, fishers nor hunters." People wanted to go places — easier and faster. Sleds got wheels, wheels got powered by cows and horses, animal power got engines, engines got motors, motors got speed, speed got faster.

Present-day bullet trains can travel at about two hundred miles per hour. The distance from Ur to Babylon was about 150 miles; a bullet train could have made the trip in about forty-five minutes, although it would have rattled the Sumerians' bronze trinkets a bit. It would have seemed to them about the same as it would seem to today's New Yorkers if rifle boring were added to the

Holland Tunnel and a few thousand commuters fired from Manhattan to Jersey City.

> *Great rats, small rats, lean rats, brawny rats,*
> *Brown rats, black rats, gray rats, tawny rats.*
> *Grave old plodders, gay young friskers,*
> *Fathers, mothers, uncles, cousins,*
> *Cocking tails and pricking whiskers,*
> *Families by tens and dozens,*
> *Brothers, sisters, husbands, wives —*
> *Followed the Piper for their lives.*
>
> —Robert Browning,
> "The Pied Piper of Hamelin"

Lily Tomlin said: "The trouble with the rat race is that even if you win you're still a rat." What's the hurry? Is *obliviosus* running *to* or *from* something? No one seems to know. No one has time to think about it — they're "kind of rushed" right now. "Got to get somewhere," you know. There are over four million miles of roads in the United States alone. The entire Roman Empire only had fifty thousand miles of road. Modern man has built so many roads, he has created a worldwide labyrinth.

It has already been suggested that *obliviosus* has forgotten what he was thinking about. Perhaps he has also forgotten where he has been and where he is going. Zoologists tell us (although you could find out for yourself, if you wanted) that spiders are nearsighted, if not blind. Consequently, nature has provided them with a single dry thread called the dragline. It helps them to keep track of where they have been and, therefore, where they are. When Theseus of Greek mythology was lost in the labyrinth, Ariadne got him out with a similar thread. *Obliviosus* does not have a dragline, although he seems to be in need of one. Maybe he lost it when he lost his tail.

In *Civilized Man's Eighty Deadly Sins,* Konrad Lorenz writes that we must ask ourselves what does more damage to the mind of modern man: his blind greed for money or his enervating haste. He offers his opinion:

> It is very probable that, beside greed for property or for higher social standing, or both, *fear* plays an essential role — fear of being overtaken in the race, fear of poverty, fear of making wrong decisions, fear of not being able to keep up with the whole nerve-racking situation. Anxiety in every form is certainly the basic factor in draining the health of modern man, causing high blood pressure, renal atrophy, cardiac infarction and other diseases. Man rushes, not because he is propelled by greed, for this alone would not induce him to ruin his own health, but because he is *driven,* and what drives him can only be fear.

If so, *obliviosus* is no better off than when he climbed the trees out of fear. No tree is tall enough, no road is long enough, no place is noisy enough, busy enough or crowded enough to escape. "We have met the enemy," Pogo says, "and they is us."

> *The illusion that times that were are better than those that are, has probably pervaded all ages.*
> — Horace Greeley

What of "the good old days"? Was life a little easier, a little better in the past? *Homo erectus,* about 500,000 B.C., lived in tribes. According to Jan Jelinek in *The Evolution of Man:* "A tribe comprised three to six adult males, six to ten adult females and fifteen to twenty children of varying ages. Therefore the group consisted of about thirty individuals.

Jericho was a village about 8000 B.C. Something like three thousand people lived in the small oasis community at a time when their contemporaries were still living in caves. Other settlements — Çatal Hüyük in Southern Anatolia, for example, only slightly less ancient — covered twice the area of the architecturally primitive Jericho. Çatal Hüyük had a population of about ten thousand.

During the Third Dynasty, about 2000 B.C., the Sumerian city of Ur was in the shape of an irregular oval, measuring a half-mile wide by three-quarters mile long. The administrative center for an irrigated district is Mesopotamia, it had an estimated population of 360,000. It is expected that the Sumerian phrase for "excuse me" was a common utterance.

The American architect Edgar Chambless designed a most ingenious city. It was to have been built like a shell around and alongside a highway. For nearly thirty years he tried to sell the idea he called Roadtown. People were not too interested, and one morning poor Edgar jumped out of his hotel window. Too soon, Edgar.

The simple life. Cool, fresh well water, sipped from a gourd or a metal dipper. Walks down the middle of a dirt road in the moonlight. Conversations by the fireside, not hurried but with many quiet spaces, the wood crackling and popping during the silences. Biscuits and cornbread, made from scratch, cooked in an oven fired by wood and eaten at a table where the food and the family were genuinely appreciated.

In the middle of the meal, a child looks up from the table and sees some men with sticks and measuring tapes, walking toward the village. "What are they doing, Poppa?" the boy asks. "I don't know, son, but they seem to be in a hurry."

PHOENIX — Freeway to run over ancient villages:
Pleas to prevent a planned freeway here from running over the relics of two Hohokam Indian villages were rejected by a federal appeals court. It agreed the West

Papago Alternative is the only "feasible and prudent" route for the last uncompleted stretch of I-10. The villages are believed to be fourteen hundred years old.
— *USA Today,* October 13, 1983

* * *

When Albert Schweitzer returned to Europe following his long travels in Africa, someone asked him: "Well, what do you think of civilization?"

"It's a good idea," Schweitzer replied. "Somebody ought to start it."

— 5 —

The Rise of Culture: From Altamira to Alice Cooper

*How can you dislike a guy who eats a tamale with
the wrapper still on it?*

— Shirley MacLaine
on Gerald Ford

In a *tres chic* restaurant in a metropolitan area, an impeccable
young man was dining with an elegant female companion. They
were in the middle of their Bananas Foster when a stranger
walked up to their table and loomed over the man.

The young man looked up at the intruder with an annoyed,
disdainful gaze. The stranger, an older man, also meticulously
dressed, spoke: "I beg your pardon. I really don't mean to
interrupt your dinner, but I saw you from across the room and I
just *knew* you were a graduate of State College."

At this recognition, the younger man put down his fork and
smiled. Winking at his companion, he said: "I know, you could
tell by my erudite look, my *bon vivant* attitude and my superior
taste in food and drink. Or maybe you could tell by my refined,
cultured manner. Or perhaps you have seen my photo in the
society pages . . ."

"No," the older man interrupted, "I just saw the 'S' on your
ring a while ago when you were picking your nose."

The word *culture* has ambience, but its definition is ambiguous. It can mean custom, growing crops, an environment of education and refinement, a stage or race of society, or something growing in a petri dish. As used here, culture will not mean custom in the habitual sense, as, for example: in many foreign countries it is customary to drive an automobile on the left-hand side of the road. In the United States, if you insist on driving on the left-hand side of the road, you won't be able to find an insurance company who will carry you.

Nor will culture, as used here, mean environment, per se, or race, per se. No matter what your race, you are subjected to the influences of your environment. Again, for example, if you're a black American born in Chicago, you will learn to speak the language you hear daily, and it is a safe bet that you won't begin speaking Bantu at an early age. Or Tupelo, Mississippian, for that matter.

Culture, for our purposes, will mean what people do, their activities and amusements. Since even this narrowed definition encompasses so much — farming, domesticity, warfare, government, law, religion, and magic, within this context the particular attempts of *obliviosus* at self-expression, self-absorption, self-discovery, self-help, self-improvement, and self-surrender deserve a look before moving on to bigger and better things.

> *All art is quite useless.*
> — Oscar Wilde, Preface
> to *The Picture of Dorian Gray*

> *Art is the most intense mode of individualism that the world has known.*
> — Oscar Wilde, *The Soul of Men Under Socialism*

The trouble with art is that some people can't make up their minds about it, even though it has been around for a long, long time. We have already viewed the paintings on the cave walls as magical images. They can also be viewed as art. At Lascaux, in the Dordogne Valley of France, ancient artists depicted many animals. Only one obscure sketch in a well shaft depicts man, and that one in a stick-figure, primitive way in comparison with the powerful and realistic horse and mammoth representations. At Altamira, in northern Spain, the pictures are more stylized and include man more frequently. Some Spanish caves depict man with bows and arrows and in hunting, fishing and dancing scenes. All cave art, in varied ways, is powerfully beautiful.

But something happened. Almost overnight on a relative scale of time (overnight being the Mesolithic period), the art, like the dinosaurs millions of years earlier, simply vanished. Europe warmed up and became climatically close to what it is today. Man still roamed, but for some reason lost the artistic impulse. For three or four thousand years cultural evolution in western Europe marked time.

Except for a few little painted pebbles, nothing much happened until the farmers across the Mediterranean to the East began to crank up their plows. When art reappeared, it was as ornamentation for practical items such as pottery, textiles and metalwork. Still later, the ornamentation again became art in itself, often separate from the utensils it had decorated.

Again it seems that *obliviosus* progresses so far, forgets what he's doing, backs up and starts over. In *Evolution in the Arts*, Thomas Munro summarizes three trends in art which are to some extent regressive and opposed to evolution. The first, he says, is catastrophic. The second is a voluntary return to simpler, more primitive types of life and art. The third is romantic primitivism as expressed in the arts of complex, civilized societies, what Herbert Spencer called "rebarbarization." The last two trends, Munro states, may have constructive effects in helping to revive lost values of an earlier age. As to the catastrophic, he says: "Where a wholesale disintegration of the collective mode of life ensues, it is inevitably destructive to complex forms of art," that is, if you consider covering Lake Erie with Saran Wrap a complex form of art.

Whether primitive, romantic or catastrophic, *obliviosus* uses the methods he has at hand in his continuing desire to dabble. A company that produces painting boxes for amateur landscape artists has the following instructions on a slip of paper enclosed in every kit: "Take the palette from the box, squeeze some paint on it from the tubes, dip your brush into the paint and daub the canvas with it." An excellent set of instructions for a method used by Rembrandt, Renoir, van Gogh and many, many others.

"I don't know art," *obliviosus* says, "but I know what I like." And so he does. Thus, he doesn't have to know what it means to know it is art. A story that has been told many times, almost never in the same way twice, is that of Picasso assisting the Paris gendarmes in catching a burglar. The great artist had seen the burglar, so he did a painting of the man and gave it to the police. Guided by the sketch, they rounded up two hundred people, a house, a hearse, a pair of old boots and a can opener. Other versions list other items, including two nuns and the Eiffel Tower.

Freud, as well as the romantics of the Enlightenment, felt that reason alone was not enough to achieve human happiness. *Obliviosus* has always sought to transcend himself and, by so doing, reconcile his primitive physical nature with the rational demands of civilization. One of the methods he uses to do this is art. The others are controlled substances. Writing on the bearing of psychoanalysis on theories of art history, Munro says:

> Art is one of the main channels of sublimation, both
> for the artist himself and for those who respond to his
> work sympathetically. It provides approved, symbolic

substitutes for repressed and condemned desires, and thus a partial satisfaction of them. It also provides a fantasy fulfillment of approved but frustrated desires, and a partial escape from the miseries of life.

It can be used to excess as a chronic evasion of responsibilities and more lastingly effective ways to improve the situation. The commercialization of "dreams for sale" can provide a numbing opiate for the public mind.

And that is the best segue imaginable for the introduction to the popular arts at hand: television and movies.

> *Am I going to be a movie star now?*
> — Elizabeth Ray

Two drunks wandered into a zoo and as they staggered past a lion's cage, the king of beasts let out a terrific roar.

"C'mon, let's get out of here," said the first drunk.

"You go ahead if you want to," replied his more inebriated buddy, while making himself comfortable on a bench. "I'm gonna stay for the movie."

The world's first photograph, a blurry picture of a courtyard in France, was taken in 1826. It didn't move. While the quality of photography steadily improved over the years, none of the pictures moved until the late nineteenth century when Edison invented the kinetoscope. By 1892, penny arcades (or peep shows, as they were wont to be called) proliferated, and people flocked in droves to see such bits of life as "What the Bootblack Saw" or "How Bridget Served the Salad Undressed," both of which brought in more gross profit than titles like "Surf at

Dover" or "Beavers at Play."

When the pennies began to flood the tills, Edison let himself be convinced that he should project his pictures so that a whole audience could view them at one time. On April 23, 1896, the first public showing was held and the paper reported the next morning: "An unusually bright light fell upon the screen. Then came into view two precious blond persons of the variety stage doing the umbrella dance with commendable celerity." In those days, any celerity — speed — was commendable.

The "flicks" caught on and immediately fostered such memorable amusements as the Pennsylvania Limited running at sixty miles an hour — directly toward the audience. It was an experience that would not be duplicated for almost sixty years, when Cinerama and 3-D appeared.

The first movies were vignettes, comic interludes, nature studies, and other tidbits of topical interest. There were no "stories" until Edwin S. Porter's *Life of an American Fireman* in 1903. Porter is better remembered for his movie, *The Great Train Robbery*, which came later. Although short and episodic, *The Great Train Robbery* is considered the first real movie. A story of crime in the old West (it was filmed in New Jersey), it concluded with a scene where one of the characters, for no reason connected with the story, draws his pistol and fires at the audience. (Anyone who has seen the movie *Grey Fox*, made in the 1980s, saw a glimpse of *The Great Train Robbery* and the audience's reaction to the final scene — they stood up and fired back.) With the Pennsylvania Limited bearing down on them and the desperadoes shooting at them, the people at the turn of the century must have been a nervous lot.

The feature film did not arrive until the appearance of the genius named David Wark Griffith and his controversial social epic, *The Birth of a Nation*, and his unappreciated spectacular, *Intolerance*. Neither has been surpassed, although the ideas of both have been imitated (*Gone With the Wind, Potemkin, The*

Gold Rush and *Greed*, to name a few).

At first, actors and actresses were unnamed. Then someone had the idea to create The Star. "The day will come," said Andy Warhol, "when everyone will be famous for fifteen minutes." Hero today and gone tomorrow. In the early days of the movies, Francis X. Bushman, Mary Pickford, Norma and Constance Talmadge, Theda Bara (originally known as Theodosia Goodman, from Ohio), and others were famous for more than fifteen minutes. They were thought of lovingly by millions of men, women and children who considered them almost as members of their own families.

In the eighties, the movies are bigger, faster and more colorful, yet seem to be generally in the same state of regression as the fine arts. There is a preponderance of repetition: movies with II, III or IV following the title, remakes of previous movies, re-releases of the previous movies, and new movies which shouldn't have been made in the first place.

For the generation of *obliviosus* which does not remember (for in most cases, to be fair, they could not have seen) the originals, it doesn't seem to make any difference. For those who did see the original *Tarzan*, *Scarface*, *Where the Boys Are*, *Breathless*, *The Postman Always Rings Twice*, or *The Blue Lagoon*, to name a few, they are likely to say, "This is where I came in."

> *Henry James was one of the nicest old ladies I ever met.*
>
> — William Faulkner

A world-famous author went to a fancy-dress ball one evening. It was, after all, a party, and he was enjoying himself. He checked his dignity at the door, wore a paper hat, tooted a horn and generally "let his hair down."

In his wanderings around the rooms where the party was being held, he came across a teenaged college girl who stared at him relentlessly. Aware of her observation, he decided to saunter over and introduce himself.

When he told the girl who he was, she took one deep breath and exclaimed, "Well, for gossakes — and you're required reading!"

From the numinous quality of the paintings on the walls of caves, made "real" by projections of active imagination in the primitive human psyche, to the luminous quality of the images on the walls of theaters, made by real projectors and requiring only passive imagination (escapism), there must always have been the need for *obliviosus* to nudge an elbow at the person next to him in order to share a particularly exciting moment. In that urge to nudge is the essence of literature: the need to communicate and, equally important for the nudgee, the need to be communicated to.

There is a tendency to consider the beginning of literature as simultaneous with the beginning of writing. By definition, literature is written expression dealing with ideas of permanent interest. When the term "recorded history" is used, it generally is understood to begin with the early inscriptions of the Sumerians and the Egyptians. The earliest written "stories" are from Homer, Hesiod and the Vedic hymns. But literature in its broadest sense must have had a long prehistoric stage that was oral, and all "stories" that have ever been "written" must certainly have found their origin in spoken language.

There are a number of theories regarding the beginning of language, but it is a fact that nobody knows for sure how language began. Charles Berlitz, who knows a great deal about language in general, admits that no one knows how it started, though he cites several theories promulgated by linguists in his book, *Native Tongues*:

— The "pooh-pooh" theory: words came as exclamations of dislike, hunger, pain or pleasure. (The first word could have been "Ow!").

— The "bow-wow" theory: words came as imitations of animal sounds, thereby naming the animals (as children still do).

— The "ding-dong" theory: words came as imitations of sounds in nature, such as "splash," "crack," or "boom."

— The "yo-he-ho" theory: words came as chants made during collective effort, as in the song of the Volga boatmen.

— The "look out!" theory: words came as warnings or threats to stay away from food, mates, possessions, or falling rocks.

Berlitz goes on to say that "language probably derived not from one but from a combination of the various sources proposed by theorists." Simple language, although useful in emergencies ("Look out! Here come a ding-dong bow-wow! Ow!), becomes literature only when it is used to delight and stir an audience.

Stories began out of imagination, using repetition for dramatic effect and objects for illustration. They began in a simple way, as directions, relating of incidents, or creation myths. They evolved into entertainments, some with morals or inspirational messages, some as national epics, and some simply humorous (or humorously simple). Since there are no tape recordings of the oral literature of the Stone Age, we must draw analogies from the stories of present-day primitives. Robert Lowie, in *An Introduc-*

tion to Cultural Anthropology, gives an example of droll humor from the Caucasus region:

> Three men from the district of Auch went traveling and came to a cave. They supposed it to be inhabited by a fox, so one of them crawled in. But it was occupied by a bear, who with a single blow tore off the intruder's head. When the man gave no sign of life at all, his two companions pulled him out and discussed his headless state, but neither could recall whether he had ever had a head. Then one of them ran to the village and asked the widow whether her husband had really at one time had a head. She answered, "I can not recollect for certain, but I do know that every year I made him a new cap."

Eventually, the songs that were sung and the tales that were told for thousands of years were written down. The first writings were pictographs, the pictures themselves symbolizing events or names. Later came symbols for syllables which could be combined to make the sounds of familiar words. Then the Phoenicians invented the first true alphabet, which consisted of letters for individual basic sounds.

One sidelight to the Phoenicians is that, although they invented the alphabet, they had almost nothing to say. They had no literature except for some of a religious nature. Instead, they used their writings for the business records of their maritime trade. In *The Long Road West*, Robert Morley tells us:

> The gift of writing as nurtured by the stay-at-home Hebrew became his means of keeping a ring of fire around his permanent faith. No equivalent excitement, no equivalent faith, is expressed in Phoenician writ-

ing. Perhaps the technological equipment which enabled the Phoenician to go where he would, inhibited other forms of self-expression.

Obliviosus has had a long and interesting history of literature: oral, written and visual. Huckleberry Finn's adventures are not so different from the adventures of Homer's heroes or those of the *Raiders of the Lost Ark*. The promotional methods may vary, however. At the 1984 annual convention of the American Booksellers Association, some of the featured guests were Raquel Welch, Rosalynn Carter, Lee Iacocca, Connie Francis and Mr. T. So much for literature.

> *I know only two tunes: one of them is "Yankee Doodle," and the other isn't.*
> — Ulysses S. Grant

Bernard Shaw went into a London restaurant for lunch one day. Soon the orchestra began to play a particularly noisy tune. Without any intermission, another cacophonous tune followed. Shaw called the headwaiter over and asked:

"Does the orchestra play anything on request?"

"Yes sir," the man replied. "Is there something you would like them to play?"

"There is," said Shaw. "Ask them to play dominoes until I have finished eating."

When the need for self-expression transcends the abilities of the spoken, written or pictured word, perhaps due to an excess of emotion, then man turns to music. Music has a long history, but most of it is shrouded in silence. Thus, historians have differing opinions as to whether music evolved as an integral part of cultural evolution or as a separate process. It is generally agreed that instrumental music evolved separately from song and opera. Schopenhauer regarded music in any form as separate from the rest of life.

The first music seems to have been instrumental, a rhythmic accompaniment for dancing. As probably, in Shaw's restaurant, when the waiter dropped a tray of dishes, everybody got up and started dancing. Later, the Greeks devised musical scales from magical numbers. Music as a separate art probably did not exist until the Middle Ages, when the Greek modal notations were adapted by the Jongleurs, Troubadours, Trouvères, Minnesingers and Meistersingers. It was during the Middle Ages that harmony was born, although some similarities existed earlier in songs with choral repetitions.

Without a long dissertation on the evolution of types of songs and symphonic modes, it can simply be said that lyrics are the literature of the heart and instrumental music is contrapuntal to silence. At their best, that is. There are good and bad examples of lyrics and of music itself. For every "As Time Goes By," there is a "Mairzy Doats." For every Mozart sonata, there is a portable radio on someone's shoulder playing the tonal equivalent of a truckload of frightened monkeys crashing through a plate-glass window into a munitions factory.

But atonal music is not limited to pop culture. At a performance of a modernistic orchestral arrangement in a sedate music hall, the instruments consisted of ten grand pianos, six xylophones, a fire-alarm siren, an airplane propeller, and several automobile horns. As the music mounted in volume, the audience became restless and grew increasingly more excitable. Finally, after about ten minutes of the composition, a man in one of the front rows raised a white handkerchief tied to his cane, and the entire audience burst into laughter.

ON EDGAR BERGEN'S LAP

A mallard whistles low over the lake. Trout break the water's surface. A wood fire crackles.

Enjoying nature's music doesn't mean you can't enjoy your own. Next time you set up your camp, set up your music, too.

> — From a magazine advertisement
> for portable AM-FM stereo
> radios with huge (eight-inch)
> bass reflex speakers

A man traveled to the Grand Canyon, arriving in time to view a gorgeous sunset. As he moved away from the crowds of people, the better to view the awesome spectacle in solitude, he found an isolated spot from which to meditate on the beauty of nature. Just as the sun began to set, changing the canyon's colors before his eyes and filling his psyche with primeval wonder caught in a moment of peace, a young couple walked up carrying a portable radio blaring the song of the frightened monkeys.

Perhaps it isn't so much that music itself is becoming more primitive, even decadent, but that it is *obliviosus* who is becoming so. A disciple of Raja Yoga said: "Most people today are afraid of silence because they don't know what to do with it." Perhaps they don't know what silence *is*. In this age of radio, television ("I just keep it on for company"), tape recorders, jet engines, automobile traffic, and other features of everyday life, the environment is saturated with the music of modern technology: just plain noise.

For those who like this sort of thing, this is the sort of thing they like.

> — Max Beerbohm

The general demeanor and tastes of a cultured civilization may be hinted at by the articles it leaves behind after its demise. Following are some of the items archeologists have unearthed, the remains of former civilizations:

— ca. 2650 B.C. (from the great death pit at Ur of the Sumerians): a delicately crafted, eighteen-inch-high, gold, lapis lazuli, shell, and silver "ram caught in a thicket."

— ca. 2450 B.C. (from the king's grave at Ur): a detailed model of a boat, in silver, twenty-five inches in length.

— ca. 2300 B.C. (from Nineveh): a beautifully sculptured, twelve-inch-high bronze head, possibly portraying Sargon of the Akkadians, one of the first monarchs to conceive a world kingdom.

— ca. 1900 B.C. (from Mohenjo Dara in the Indus Valley): a realistic bronze sculpture, four and one-quarter inches high, of a Harappan dancing girl.

— ca. 600 B.C. (from Persia): a beautiful silver-and-gold winged ibex, eleven inches high.

Here are some of the items that present-day *obliviosus* will leave behind for the archeologists of the future to dig up, along with probable interpretations of them:

— A hollow aluminum cylinder with a pair of tri-angular openings at one end, printed with the name *Coors*, an unknown word.

— A plastic case containing a reel of plastic tape. Purpose of the tape unknown, probably used for measuring. The case is imprinted with the words "Alice Cooper," evidently the owner of the device.

— A box with a glass window and two appendages: one a cord of some type with a prong at the end, the other an extendable metallic arm with a piece of aluminum foil attached. Obviously a child's pull-toy.

— A keyboard of some type with a cable attached and the button marked "delete" jammed into the on position. Probably a weapon, as the obsolete word *delete* then meant to destroy.

— An object of fabricated material, woven with plasticized threads of several colors. Either a leisure suit of the era, or the seat covers from a 1939 Dodge.

— A collarless, short-sleeved cotton shirt imprinted with the word *foxy*. Apparently the name of a team involved in some form of sport.

* * *

A shipwrecked mariner had spent several years on a deserted South Sea island. Then one bright morning he was thrilled to see a ship offshore and a boat pulling out for his island. When the boat grounded on the beach, the officer in charge threw the marooned sailor a bundle of newspapers, yelling: "The captain's compliments. Read through these and let us know if you still want to be rescued."

– 6 –

Not Tonight,
I've Got a Program

"We are lost!" the captain shouted
As he staggered down the stairs.
                                        — James T. Fields,
                                   The Ballad of the Tempest

It was the middle of the evening, the kids were in bed and the
husband was watching television, his feet up on an ottoman and a
beer in his hand. Other than the sound of the set, it was quiet.

He felt the light touch of a hand on his neck and looked up as
his wife sat on the arm of his chair and snuggled close to him. She
leaned down, her face close to his, and whispered in his ear,
"Let's have a little fun tonight."

"OK," he replied. "I'm gonna watch *Monday Night Football*.
I'll leave the porch light on for you when I go to bed."

A survey taken in the United States five years ago found that
Americans spend three-fourths of their leisure time in front of the
television set. A list of leisure-time activities ranked TV Viewing
as #1 at 72 percent, while Engaging in Sexual Activities ranked
#14 at 11 percent. Working in the Garden ranked higher at 22
percent — there has to be some Freudian parallel with Adam and
Eve in that statistic.

The Love Boat has sunk. *That's Incredible.* Anyone who cares should go to *Dallas* for about *60 Minutes* and have a *Hart to Hart* talk with someone in the television *Dynasty*. Ask *Gloria* for *Matt Houston*, Mr. *Newhart*, or one of the *Jeffersons*, and be there from *9 to 5*. If you're a sexually deprived person, you may want to *M*A*S*H* someone's nose when you find him. After you do that, go over to *Archie Bunker's Place* on *Falcon Crest* for a *Magnum P.I.* of champagne to celebrate. But it won't change anything. You'll still be the *Fall Guy* with the *Hill Street Blues*, finding that *Three's Company* (the third being the television set) and, though your heart may feel like a *Football*, you might as well give up and watch a *Movie*. (The titles in italics represent the thirty most popular programs viewed by men and women over eighteen, as revealed in a survey about four months after the "TV Tops Sex" survey. All the programs listed in the survey are used above, eight having appeared on both the male and female viewer lists, with movies represented three times.)

At the time of this survey, these shows made screenplay seven times more popular than foreplay. In the past, although there were no comparative surveys, the shows might have been *The $64,000 Question, My Little Margie*, or *Gunsmoke*; in the future, they might be *J.R. Meets Mr. Rogers on Ork, Shootout at the Pentagon Corral*, or *Bikini Beach XXXIV*. The point is, *obliviosus* is interested in sex, but mainly out of curiosity. Is anyone going to do anything about this obvious affront to human reproduction? You bet your Nielsen. The following article appeared in a magazine about a year after these two surveys:

By the time you read this, MCA, the giant entertainment conglomerate north of Hollywood, may be eager to publicize *Love Skills*, an hour-long but timeless education tape for home video. It was originated to instruct the cassette-buyers in the basics of human sexuality, including lessons in anatomy, sex relations, foreplay and fantasy.

Good. Before TV, all we had were the streets.

If you read a lot of books, you're considered well-read. But if you watch a lot of TV, you're not considered well-viewed.

— Lily Tomlin

Television is a subject without a correlate in the history of *obliviosus*. Mankind has always enjoyed viewing sunlight, moonlight, starlight and firelight. According to the statistics, we now seem to enjoy viewing artificial light, as well. Perhaps in Edison's day, when the invention was new, a lot of people sat around and stared at light bulbs, but it is not likely that they all did it at once and even less likely that they did it for very long.

On April 9, 1984, an estimated 500 million viewers watched (for three and one-half hours) the Academy Award presentations. At no other time in the long history of the world have 500 million people — all at the same time — viewed the same work of art, read the same book, or listened to the same song. *Obliviosus* has been around for tens of thousands of years, and until less than four hundred years ago there were not 500 million people in the whole world.

Far Out!
— Slightly antiquated expression describing anything incomprehensible

If William Blake were alive today, his poem might read: "TV! TV! Burning bright/ In the forests of the night." An interesting book on the effects of staring into the darkness at a box of light is *Four Arguments for the Elimination of Television*, written by a man whose name sounds like a political map, Jerry Mander. The

75

book is a total departure from previous writing about television. It argues the physical effects of television on viewers, its confinement of experience, the degree of its economic control, and its undemocratic nature. Mander says:

> When you are watching television the major thing you are doing is looking at light. For four [now over seven] hours a day, human beings sit in dark rooms, their bodies stilled, gazing at light. Nothing like this has ever happened before.
>
> Sitting in darkened rooms, with the natural environment obscured, other humans dimmed out, only two senses operating, both within a very narrow range, the eyes and the other body functions stilled, staring at light for hours and hours, the experience adds up to something nearer to sense deprivation than anything that has come before it.
>
> Television isolates people from the environment, from each other, and from their own senses. When you are watching TV, you are experiencing mental images. As distinguished from most sense-deprivation experiments these mental images are not yours. They are someone else's. Because the rest of your capacities have been subdued, and the rest of the world dimmed, these images are likely to have an extraordinary degree of influence. There is no question but that someone is speaking into your mind and wants you to do something.
>
> First, keep watching.
> Second, carry the images around in your head.
> Third, buy something.
> Fourth, tune in tomorrow.

I'm being punished. Nothing electronic for two weeks.

— Little boy to friend.

More on Big Brother later. What about little brother and little sister? What effect does television have on the children of *obliviosus*? In a 1982 essay in *Newsweek*, Joshua Meyrowitz related a conversation he overheard in a restaurant. A woman and a young boy were in the next booth. "So, how have you been?" the woman asked. The boy — who could not have been more than seven or eight years old — replied, "Frankly, I've been feeling a little depressed lately."

Meyrowitz went on to say that children are acting more like adults and adults, conversely, have begun acting like children. He points out that it is not unusual to see children wearing suits and designer dresses, while adults wear Mickey Mouse T-shirts, jeans and sneakers.

Are children growing up too fast? Depends on how — or when — you look at it. Philippe Ariès, the French cultural historian from whom we have already heard on the subject of death, also wrote a book titled *Centuries of Childhood*, in which he stated that childhood and adolescence as we know them are inventions peculiar to modern times. He wrote, "Under the Old Regime, as soon as the child could live without the constant solicitude of his mother, his nanny or his cradle-rocker, he belonged to adult society."

Ariès got a lot of criticism for his viewpoint, and society thought it fixed that problem. There are people alive today who remember when children six, seven and eight years old worked ten to twelve hours a day in a factory. Society fixed that, too. Now children are made aware of present social values through the expediency of television. As Yogi Berra said, "You can see a lot just by looking," and what the children see is that life is made up primarily of jiggle, jangle, jerks and junk.

For children, television is an educational experience, even if it is "a little depressing." For adults (which is what the twenty or more million children under six who watch television twenty to thirty hours a week are going to grow up to be), television is visual thumbsucking.

> *All I had to do was keep turning left.*
> — Winner of the 1946
> Indianapolis 500

Another problem with television is that children sitting in front of it do not get enough exercise. Or at least that *used* to be a problem. Now, when they have been sitting still for too long, they can walk up to the arcade and play video games. The amount of exercise involved is directly proportionate to the distance from the house to the arcade.

Yes, they're playing a new game in River City, and it starts with *V* and that stands for Video. A video game, unlike Monopoly or Scrabble, is not a group, or social, game. It is one-on-one with a machine. Instead of competing with another person, it's more like challenging your blender to a duel. It is a substitute for true play. The essayist Margaret Logan wrote in *Boston Review*: "The machine's demands — its pace, its fixed program — virtually eliminate daydreaming, invention, and fantasy, all cited by Freud, Erikson, and others as significant benefits of true play [and] the exploratory play that Einstein believed was fundamental to productive scientific thought."

If there seems to be something missing in this computerized playmate/opponent situation, it is in the area of physical involvement — utilization of the senses. After all, the arcade games are only TV with a button to poke or a handle to twist, which may lead to a genetic mutation of "E.T." fingers and "Hulk" wrists.

But, as Mighty Mouse used to say, "Here I come to save the day." The industry, according to a market research firm in Connecticut, will soon stimulate the neglected senses. Or at least the video game player will soon be able to feel and smell what is going on. Evidently, they have not figured out how to satisfy the sense of taste as yet, unless that is covered under "poor."

For a dollar a play, in an enclosed booth, the smell of burning tires, popcorn, freshly cooked pizzas and other substances will emanate from the computer. Seats will vibrate to simulate the feeling of space travel. Consoles will come complete with seat belts and controls that are operated with feet, hips, biceps and even eye movements. And if someone unplugs the machine while you're playing, presumably you'll die.

Death and destruction seem to be the punishment for failure in most video games, sarcastically represented by electronic yells, squeals, moans or whimpers. According to a newspaper item:

> A recent video game called "Fireman-Fireman" seems to be cashing in on the public's taste for the macabre: its object is to position a safety net on the screen to catch babies falling from a burning building. The more babies a player saves, the higher the score. With every miss, a tiny baby splats on the "ground" and a little angel appears in a corner. Three angels [and splats] and you're out.

Whether or not that game is still around, and if developing proficiency at video games seems to be a waste of time for the youngsters, consider the following article from a newspaper, which appeared a couple of years following the above report:

> HUNTSVILLE, Ala. — The Army is spending thirty million dollars to develop a cheap missile that

can be guided to battlefield targets by ground troops using television screens and joy stick controllers in what amounts to a deadly video game.

To select a target, the operator simply uses a pistol-grip joy stick to maneuver bright cursors over the TV image and pulls a trigger. The computer does the rest. [Splat!]

But we don't want to get ahead of ourselves. Let's leave the kids to their training and rejoin them later, when we talk about war.

> *We're in the same position as a plumber laying a pipe. We're not responsible for what goes through the pipe.*
>
> — David Sarnoff

A person who does not own, rent, borrow, steal, or in some way possess and watch a television set is considered a social outcast, perverted, deranged, an anathema to society to be shunned like a rat carrying the plague. This person is automatically — and suddenly, not to mention rudely — eliminated from any conversation that begins with "Did you watch . . . ?"

Doris Lessing provides an excellent summary of the phenomena of television as it relates to culture in her book *Briefing for a Descent into Hell*. She comments on watching television for a few hours one evening. Based on that experience, she concluded that the most outstanding characteristic of twentieth-century civilization is that all events are equally important, whether war, a game, the weather, the craft of plant-growing, a fashion show, or a police hunt. She also remarks that for a culture so remarkably advanced in some ways, it is even more remarkably backward in others.

ON EDGAR BERGEN'S LAP

* * *

Airline Pilot to Stewardess: "When we get to Denver, how about joining me for a cozy weekend in a quiet downtown hotel?"

Stewardess: "Well, Captain, it would seem that certain illuminating knowledge garnered from among a plethora of psychoanalytical studies, as well as an awareness of your pejorativeness in the more esoteric aspects of sexual behavior preclude you from such erotic confrontation."

Pilot: "I don't get it."

Stewardess: "That's what I said."

He Doesn't Have
A Personality,
He Has a Syndrome

*I didn't know until I was fifteen that there was
anything in the world except me.*

— F. Scott Fitzgerald

A woman was talking to her friend about the demise of her
latest relationship.

"I don't want to say he was a loser, Mary, but he had to be
retrained when he came back from coffee break. He made four
enemies at a Dale Carnegie class. He spilled Raid on his pants
and his fly died. He bought a suit with two pairs of pants and
burned a hole in the coat. He drank so much he saw Disneyland
three years before it was built. He tried bath oil beads — he said
they taste all right, but they don't have the same effect as a bath.
He got a double hernia from a typographical error in a sex
manual. On our first date, he parked the car and put his hand on
my knee. I said, 'You can go farther than that.' He started the car
and drove thirty miles to the next town. He . . ."

"Excuse me," Mary interrupted. "If he was *that* bad, why did
you go with him for so long?"

"Well," she answered, "my real man wasn't ideal, but my
ideal man isn't real."

Seeking perfection in self and in others, *obliviosus* has beaten a path to the door of psychology, expecting to be issued a neat package of personal development: Body Language, Mind Control, Face-Reading, Handwriting-Reading (Graphology), Depth Psychology, Reflexology, Numerology. Rollo May, T-A, I'm OK — Who Are They?, Primal Screams, Interpret Dreams, Diet Schemes. Group Therapy, Zone Therapy, Dance Therapy, Logotherapy, Will Therapy, Won't Therapy. Est, Rest, Go West. Dare to be Great, Care to Relate?

A simple package will not work for everyone. Each individual needs various methods at different times. For example, try to use Relaxation Therapy when you're speeding down the entrance ramp to the freeway and the steering wheel comes off in your hands.

Granted, most, if not all, personal development programs work for many people. It's just that there are other methods or alternatives, although a fanatic devotee of a particular discipline would lead you to think otherwise. Arica, one of the "methods" of development, founded by a Bolivian, is a training program meant to develop a spiritual path in the body by bringing energy from the head into the *kath*, a place four inches below the navel, the midpoint of the body and the key place for Eastern martial arts. According to Jerry Rubin, "A person with consciousness in his *kath* is in control of himself." While that may be true, you can get the same effect of consciousness in your *kath* by eating a can of pork and beans.

In 1971, a man called Baba Ram Dass (who used to be called Richard Alpert before he went to India and was given wisdom, enlightenment and a new name) wrote a book called *Be Here Now*. Now, Baba/Richard, where else *could* you be? Almost everyone wants to be somewhere else, but you have to be here now even to wish it. As the man said when the husband caught him in the wife's bedroom closet, "Everybody's got to be someplace." Of course, if you ingest psychedelics for five or six years, as many of Baba's readers did in the 60s, you may come to wonder where "here" is. It was not so much "Who am I?" as it was "Where am I?" Their idea of an economy flight to Mexico was a drop of LSD on a tamale.

In the 80s, the escape devices are milder, though more pervasive throughout society. Psychologists have built so many roads to self-discovery that *obliviosus* is once again caught in the maze without a dragline. Given all of the disciplines (fads?) listed earlier (and there were/are many more), perhaps what is really needed is simplicity. Apparently, that need has been recognized, if not completely satisfied, by the method related in the following newspaper report:

> Are analyst's bills shrinking your wallet as well as your psyche? "Walk-a-Shrink," the psychiatrist on tape, may be your answer. At six dollars, the cassette is cheaper than a human therapist and supplies everything but the couch. It features the voice of creator Stanley Mulfeld asking typical questions posed by therapists, followed by pauses of twenty to forty-five seconds to allow for the listener's answers.
>
> Side 1, entitled "Uh-Huh," begins with "Just tell me how you feel," and goes on to such queries and comments as, "Mmmmm," "Why do you think that is?" "Yes," "Why did you stop?" "Uh-Huh," and "Is that what you really want?" There's more of the same on side 2, which is entitled "Yes, go on," and ends with, "That's all we have time for now."

In psychology, as in many other things, before any answer can be found the right question must be asked. In the fifth edition of his textbook *Psychology*, Norman L. Munn discusses an example of catatonic schizophrenia: "A psychiatrist who was giving a clinic could not get the patient to speak. He had actually not spoken for ten years. The doctor turned to the class saying, 'This patient has not spoken for ten years,' whereupon the patient said, 'What did you want me to say?' "

> *rood eciffo ruoy rettel ot ereh ma I*
> — Sign painter to man in
> glass-enclosed office

A simple reason for there being no simple answer is that the process of perception varies from individual to individual. The way a person sees things is a prime factor of personality. *Not* seeing things is important as well, for, otherwise, *obliviosus* would be bombarded with more stimuli than he could handle.

For example, there is something everyone sees continuously the entire time that the eyes are open. It's as plain as the nose on your face. It *is* the nose on your face. But we have learned to "erase" this object from our conscious viewing attention. Even when you look down to see your upper lip you don't "notice" the nose. If you want to "see" how much of the viewing field it takes up, close either eye and look around.

Even before Plato let that guy out of his chains in the allegory of the cave, there have been those who saw things differently, especially significant when the different view was the right one. When Copernicus said that the earth went around the sun, and not the reverse, there must have been at least one person who said, "Sure, Copernicus, you're right and the whole world is wrong."

As important as how the world or another person is perceived — perhaps more immediately important — is how *obliviosus* perceives himself. In a magazine article, a psychologist related an anecdote of a woman patient who complained that she had become nervous and fretful because life had grown too hectic: too much partying, too many late hours, long weekends, etc. "Why don't you stop?" the therapist asked. The patient stared blankly, then asked in amazement, "You mean I don't *have* to do what I *want* to do?"

> *Pies like mother used to bake before she took to whiskey and cigarettes.*
>
> — Sign in a restaurant

At a christening, the new preacher was bent on making a good impression on the parents. As he was going through the procedure, he kept up a patter of praise, predicting a great future for the infant: "Why, this child looks fine enough to become another Einstein, another Shakespeare . . . maybe even another Alexander the Great or a Napoleon!" He hesitated a moment, then asked "Ah . . . by the way, what is the baby's name?"

"Mary Ann," the mother replied.

Without getting into women's liberation, or what some more appropriately call women's rights, it is enough to say that the problem of equality really rests with the way people tend to lump a group together within a particular label — any label, as long as it covers preconceived notions. Yet there has to be some method of categorizing, so that at least our *individual* differences, sex aside, can be appreciated.

One way to categorize is to test, and one type of test is the sense-of-humor test developed by a team of California psychologists. The test operates on the premise that what we laugh at is tied to our personalities. The test consists of ten categories of humor: nonsense, philosophical, social satire, ethnic, sexual, scatological, hostile, degrading to men, degrading to women, and sick. It includes such jokes as:

> A blind man with a guide dog enters a department store, picks up his dog by the tail and swings it around in a circle over his head. A clerk hurries over and asks, "May I help you, sir?"
> The blind man replies, "No thanks, I'm just looking around."

According to the psychologists, such "sick" jokes do not necessarily appeal to people with sadistic or insensitive natures, but rather to those who are "impulsive, enthusiastic, cheerful, frank and expansive." Jokes that degrade men and women fit the personality characteristic "tough poise," people who tend to be aloof and who believe stereotypes of the opposite sex are true. People who laugh at philosophical jokes tend to be secure in their beliefs and, since they can laugh at themselves and the human condition, may have the healthiest sense of humor.

> *Anybody who goes to see a psychiatrist ought to have his head examined.*
> — Samuel Goldwyn

The suggestion that there can be a simple package or a universal answer to the psychological problems of *obliviosus* smacks of holism. A holistic approach considers behavior to be understandable only in the context of the total person, operating within a particular environment. If this is so, the question that needs to be asked is how can you readily discern the personality traits that affect both your actions and your relationships with others? The answer seems to be that there is no one answer, no simple "package of personal development" or single "personality type," although, as we have seen, there have been many attempts to package, type and label same.

Ever since Neanderthal man ran into Cro-Magnon, people have been typing other people. As long as people find types necessary to their understanding of themselves and others, the types or labels ought to be rather simple. One simple method used in recent times is astrological signs: "Hi! My name is Aloysius. I'm a Leo . . . what sign were you born under?" Anyone who is greeted in that manner, especially in a singles bar, would do well to respond "Rooms for Rent."

As if the day you were born will immediately define your personality, tell what kind of parent you would be, and whether or not you could be trusted with a joint back account! But astrology is only one of many such shortcuts to experience. At one time phrenology — the measurement of lumps and bumps on the skull — was in vogue, almost like sheep's liver divination. Today, the proprietor would ask you to leave a singles bar while you were still in one piece if you went around running your fingers over everyone's head.

One of the more famous methods of measuring the topology of types (sometimes called typology, especially when you're in a hurry) is that of the psychologist Carl Jung. His seminal work on the subject, *Psychological Types*, delineates various personality types — certain tendencies, potentials and orientations that are shared with others of the same type. What any specific person does with his or her tendencies, potentials or orientations is a question of individual psychology.

Attempts have been made to refine, define, and otherwise make more useful to everyday *obliviosus* the method that took Jung over six hundred pages to explain. In 1977, a book entitled *Psychetypes*, by Michael Malone, attempted to give a popular rendition of the method. A little later, in 1983, the Myers-Briggs

Type Indicator (MBTI) appeared. It is a refinement of Jung's theory used by many clinical psychologists. Even Eric Berne's *Games People Play*, which appeared in the 1960s, although more interested in transactions between types, still typed the individuals involved in the transactions.

Well, it seems as though it has all been said. And, as far as we know, it probably has, but people still ask "What sign are you?" ignoring the more comprehensive methods of determining personality types. Why is this so? Probably because *obliviosus* finds it too complicated to remember the complex combinations of factors. In *Psychetypes* we have the same Jungian types, but with labels like "Feeling Volcanic," "Intuitive Aethereal," "Feeling Oceanic," and "Thinking Territorial" — all either "Continuous" or "Discontinuous." If you happen to be one of the many people who cannot say *aethereal* without provoking laughter in those around you, you may wish to move on to the MBTI, where you will find labels for sixteen types, identified as ESTP, ISFP, ESTJ, INFJ, etc. In *Games People Play*, you will find types such as Sulks, Jerks, Squares and Prigs playing games labeled WAHM (Why does this always happen to me?), SWYMD (See what you made me do!), and TAGAWI (Try and get away with it).

As the attempts to type become more complicated, even if only because of the number of "simple interpretations" involved, it is no wonder that *obliviosus* reverts to the astrological "sign" tag. There are only twelve of those, they relate to the common experience of birthdays, and most people are really interested only in the ones that are the same as theirs, complementary, or incompatible, which limits it to three or four signs that it is necessary to be familiar with.

What *obliviosus* needs is a simpler method of using the Jungian system of personality types. Empirical proof of that need is contained in the fact that no one has ever walked up to someone in a singles bar and said, "Hi! My name is Aloysius. I'm an Intuitive Aethereal Jerk with tendencies toward INTP." (TAGAWI!)

Eddie Fisher married to Elizabeth Taylor is like me trying to wash the Empire State Building with a bar of soap.

— Don Rickles

Since one of the main reasons for typing people, at least in the popular sense, is to find how compatible or complementary they are, the following simplified, handy, new and improved method of personality typing is, as you may have expected, offered:

The Personality Identification Testing System (The PITS)

Objective: To determine personality type of subject, objectively.
Method: Application of the *Homo obliviosus* Test System to Uncover Frauds and Failures (HOT STUFF).

Continuing to use the singles bar analogy throughout the test, one of the following types will be determined:

Feeling Type: interested in your feelings.
Thinking Type: interested in your thoughts.
Intuitive Type: interested in your psyche.
Sensation Type: interested in your body.

Any of these types can have either an introverted or an extroverted attitude, which means that the wording for the interests above is exact for extroverts, while, for the introvert, you must substitute *his* or *her* for *your* in order to be exact. Introversion is not to be confused with selfishness; it is, instead, the way the subject perceives things.

91

All people have a primary function which is their strongest trait. One of the two functions adjacent to the primary is the secondary, or supplemental, function (shown on the chart below). The function opposite the primary function is the inferior function, the weakest trait of the person.

THE FUNCTIONS

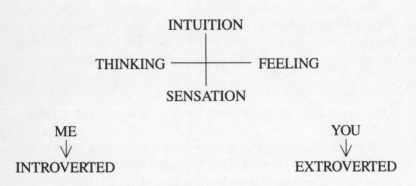

These are basic types, but we must remember that any individual can possess or lack various traits, such as will power, emotion, manual dexterity, or money. These subordinate traits will be learned only through experience. To determine the basic type, simply administer the HOT STUFF test:

Homo obliviosus Test System to Uncover Frauds and Failures:

When you approach, or are approached by, the subject, quickly perform three operations to determine type — make one observation and ask two questions:

1) Watch subject's eyes. If they look directly at you, subject is extroverted. If they cross (at any time, but especially after you ask the following question), subject is introverted.

2) Ask the simple question: "What do you think about mauve drapes in a green Chevy van?" Type will be determined by one of the following responses:
   a. Drops, spills, or spits out drink: Feeling Type.
   b. Begins answer with, "Well . . .": Thinking Type.
   c. Says "Huh?" about thirty seconds after the question: Sensation Type.
   d. Interrupts and begins to answer question before you finish asking it: Intuitive Type.

Example: Subject's eyes are looking directly at you. You ask the first question and subject interrupts you with "Well . . ." Subject is an extroverted intuitive thinking type who will say "Huh?" to the bartender in about thirty seconds.

The second question? Ask the subject if he or she is wealthy. If the answer is no, move on to next subject.

* * *

"Are you from Mars?" she asked the little man.
"Yeah," he answered.
"Are you all green like that?"
"Yeah."
"You all got antennas sticking out of your ears like that?"
"Yeah."
"You all got little round black caps in the middle of your head like that?"
"Only the orthodox."

– 8 –

Jockey Shorts and Gold Chains: The Battle of the Sexes

I have always regarded myself as a pillar in my life.
— Meryl Streep

My greatest strength is that I have no weaknesses.
— John McEnroe

"Harry," said the man to his friend at lunch, "I have a problem with my wife."

"I can't believe it," said Harry. "I've met your wife and she is intelligent, likeable, and very, very attractive."

"Oh, she's all that, all right. That's not the problem. You see, she's a nut on health and beauty aids. She spends half of every evening removing her daily makeup, putting on and taking off mudpacks, and covering herself with all kinds of oils, lotions and creams."

"Well," the friend said, "it works. She *is* very beautiful."

"Yes, she's beautiful," replied the husband, "but she keeps squirting out of my arms and sliding out of bed."

Hard on the heels of the search for self-discovery comes the quest for self-improvement. No matter what raw material *obliviosus* has to begin with, he or she will never be content as long as there is anyone around who is younger, thinner, stronger, healthier, happier, or more attractive.

Sometimes the desire for self-improvement can take different paths. One of the main diversions occurs between men and women, and, as a result of this, a certain polarity has developed between the sexes, currently known as Liberated Woman and Macho Man. Not that the polarity is new; Jessie Bernard, in her book *The Sex Game*, takes it back to the fifth day of creation. But aside from fertilization and ovulation — important enough in themselves, although reproduction is possible without mating — there must be a more basic reason for the separateness of the sexes.

An interesting account that may present the polarity in a way that answers a lot of questions comes to us in a story concerning the ancient Greek comic poet, Aristophanes. He and Socrates and a few other guys got together at Agathon's house in 416 B.C. to have a little party, which Plato writes about in his *Symposium*.

The topic of discussion was love, and when it was his turn to speak, Aristophanes explained love by relating the story of man's creation. At first, he said, there were three sexes: man, woman, and a combination of both (at that time known as Hermaphrodite, now called Unisex). All three versions were round, with four arms, four legs, four ears, one head with two faces, and a pair of the appropriate sexual accoutrements.

He went on to say that these creatures were very strong and had great ambitions. So great that they began to attack the gods. The gods, not known to tolerate such upstarts, fretted about what to do to contain these people. Zeus finally came up with a scheme. "I will tell you what I'll do," he said. "I will slice each of them down through the middle."

By doing so, he made the humans weaker, but there were more of them to do the work. Zeus also threatened to slice them again if they didn't behave, so that they would hop around on one leg. With some tucks and shapings, he split all the people to make two-legged, one faced, two-eared, etc., creatures.

According to Aristophanes, ever since then each of the halves has been running around as fast as it can on only two legs trying to find its other half. Later in the discussion, Socrates disagrees as to the basis of love and attributes it to a search for beauty . . . not as interesting a story, but a subject we should consider later.

> *Women want us to be two different people at the same time. They're looking for somebody who's John D. Rockefeller at the office and Dr. Benjamin Spock at the dinner table.*

> *I want a man I can watch TV with and also belch with. With Sam, I could watch TV, but it was really hard to belch in front of him. With Jerry I could belch, but we couldn't watch TV together.*
>
> — Responses to a survey by William Novack, author of *The Great American Man Shortage and Other Roadblocks to Romance*

While Aristophanes may have been right in his allegorical explanation, it seems that the real problem is that there are not enough sexes. The two available — the one you are and that other one — cannot perform all of the necessary functions. In *The Sex Game*, Bernard says that division into subsexes has been necessary. Even in Aristophanes' time, the Greeks had Hetaerae for companionable pleasure, concubines for their "daily needs," and wives to give them children and to take care of the house which last should be further subdivided — or subsexed — into mothers, cooks, maids and slaves.

According to Bernard, "The fact that a modern woman has to perform so many of these different functions by herself has been cited as one of her major problems." She goes on to say that much of the confusion in roles today is as much a matter of confusion between intrasex roles as between male and female roles.

The confusion is not limited to the female. Bernard divides the male collectively into three major subsexes: the Dionysian, the Parallelist, and the Assimilationist. She establishes as a criterion for classifying male subsexes the fact that the masculine mystique depends on distance. Dionysian males are "blond beasts" who go in for wenching but avoid responsible relationships. This type is also embodied in the tough-guy type, the James Bond type, the Rip Van Winkle type (sleep is as good an escape from responsibility as any), and the hobo type.

Bernard classifies (always type type, eh, Bernard?) the Parallelist males as those who want women around but who keep them at varying distances. The Assimilationist male identifies girls as "one of the boys." "The Dionysian subsex is too centripetal for most women, the Assimilationist, too centrifugal," she says. "The Parallelists insist on their sexual autonomy. But they can take, even with pleasure, the presence of women. They never lose their awareness of sexuality, in themselves or in women, but they are not afraid of it. Some of their best friends, they will concede, are women."

How does one keep up with all of the types, labels and subsexes involved in the Battle of the Sexes? There is no one simple answer, but one simple consideration to keep in mind is to ask what one really wants out of a relationship — or life, for that matter — then as Rocky Balboa says, "Go for it!" *Obliviosus* always has, and has always thought that the present situation involved in going for it is worse than any previous situation.

"We've come a long way, baby . . . and buddy." Aside from racing to find a parking place at the singles bar, a man really

doesn't have to "do battle" to win the hand of a "fair maid."
Aside from occasionally thawing out a meal of Lean Cuisine,
today's woman doesn't have to worry about some of the domestic
chores that were reported in "The Good Wife," an essay written
in the late fourteenth century covering such topics as "Three
reasons a man leaves home," "How to rid a house of fleas
('always use clean white sheets so you can see them'), flies and
mosquitoes," and "Recipe for a dinner served in thirty-one
dishes and six courses" (prepared between cleaning the chimney
and fixing the roof, it is supposed).

Today we have Jockey underwear for women (as the ad says:
"The same terrific panty that used to be only for him" —
although not many men have ever asked the store clerk for a pair
of Jockey panties) and after-shave lotion for women ("Apply it
right through your pantyhose").

Men have borrowed from women, too, in the world of fashion.
They wear gold neckchains to look macho; then they don more
jewelry, coat themselves with lotion, dye their hair, and brighten
up their wardrobes with day-glo colors often enough to be the
center of attention (in more ways than one) were they to be
somehow transported through time to join a meeting of the
ancient Greeks.

> *It's a good thing that beauty is only skin deep, or I'd
> be rotten to the core.*
>
> — Phyllis Diller

> *What's in a name? A 35% markup.*
> — Department Store Manager

Beauty (the obvious type, not the philosophical kind) comes in
two forms: the body and what is put on the body. Taking the

second first, things that are put on the body are cosmetics, clothes and adornments. Due to the messages received from men, the media, and the "beauty" industry, the prime users of cosmetics are women. According to Elissa Melamed in her book *Mirror Mirror, the Terror of Not Being Young*, "Our first line of defense is the bottles and jars. We buy oceans of lotions, cleansers, toners, exfoliants, pore refiners, masques, and gels. If all the creams were spread in one continuous layer, it would moisturize the Sahara."

Men, who fear "softening" more than "uglyfying," have not been as much of a target for the cosmetics industry as women. In fact, men are sometimes responsible for sending women ambivalent signals that directly contradict the messages of those who manufacture the magic potions women buy to ward off ugliness. In 1779, a British Act of Parliament decreed:

> All women, of whatever age, rank, profession, or degree who shall, after this Act, impose upon, seduce and betray into marriage any of His Majesty's subjects by virtue of scents, paints, cosmetic washes, artificial teeth or false hair, iron stays, bolstered hips, or high heeled shoes, shall incur the penalty of the law now in force against witchcraft and like misdemeanors.

The cosmetics industry is not selling creams, lotions and perfumes. It is preying on fear and selling dreams. Shame on you, *obliviosus*. Wash your face and smile — the joke is *on* you.

Gilda Radnor once said, "I base most of my fashion taste on what doesn't itch." Many men feel that women have it better when it comes to clothes. More comfortable, don't you know. The women don't have to wear suits that bind and ties that choke, don't have to be as "constricted." They can wear light summer dresses in the hot months while men have to wear jackets to the office.

On the surface, that may appear to be true, but there is much beneath the surface. As the psychiatrist Edmund Bergler says in *Fashion and the Unconscious*, "Pseudo-active (though really infantile) attitudes toward woman's dress explain what anthropologists have observed without being able to explain: concealment affords a greater stimulus than revelation." And concealed beneath the "light summer dress" that men think is so comfortable are so many other items — panty girdle, pantyhose, panty shield, slip, safety pins, band-aids, and other miscellaneous items — that it's a good thing a fire doesn't start from the inside.

It is a common belief, especially among men, that male clothing really doesn't change that much, doesn't follow stylish trends to the degree that women's wear does. While it is true that changes in the cut of men's clothing may evolve in a less dramatic way over longer periods of time, the differences can be better seen in the accessories.

At one time, canes were in fashion. You don't see these anymore except with drill instructors and very old men. The wearing of hats is a more noticeable difference. In nineteenth-century photographs, for example — even of men working in a factory — every man is wearing a hat of some type. It seems that no one went bareheaded. Today, not only do fewer men wear hats, the ones that do have replaced the elegant bowlers, straw skimmers, top hats and fedoras with little plastic baseball caps with a sign on the front saying "Damn, I'm Good."

Jewelry is the favorite choice of body adornments, although some cultures have used scarring, foot-binding, and other mutilations of the body as adornments in themselves. The remains of ancient gravesites prove that jewelry has been in decorative use since the beginnings of *obliviosus*.

The use of adornments was by no means limited to women. As men today wear gold chains around their necks, men of antiquity also used decorative items. Not part of a distinctive stylistic group, but very ornate and beautiful, for example, are items of Slavonic jewelry used by men from about the fifth through the ninth century A.D. The costumes of the warriors were held together by straps, which occasioned the use of finely engraved and jeweled buckles, strap-ends, and scabbard fastenings. The only vestige of this in men's accessories today is a bronzed Coors belt buckle.

An interesting period in women's jewelry was the Victorian era. Mourning the dead (are you still there, Emmeline?) may seem to be an unusual topic for the subject of jewelry, but it was a big item from the seventeenth century up to the nineteenth. It reached its peak in Victorian times and did not subside until the love brooch became fashionable in 1887.

Mourning just about everyone who died and everything bad that happened, women were seen in public wearing black bombazine dresses and jet jewelry, sometimes called black amber, a form of fossilized driftwood. Shaped in various ways into necklaces, rings, earrings, brooches, pendants and lockets, jet jewelry had all the radiance you would expect from peat bog.

During the same period, jewelry also performed memento service, primarily in the form of hair jewelry. Brooches, lockets, rings and pendants contained snips or locks of hair from the deceased. Even bracelets woven from the hair of a dead relative were worn, or, in the case of men's jewelry, the hair was woven into a cord and used as a watch chain. In order to make the hair more durable or to give it a firmer finish, horsehair was worked into the composition. Some wag certainly must have wondered which he was memorializing, Uncle Horace or Uncle's Horse.

I don't want to say my wife is spiteful, but she tried to commit suicide by eating six loaves of white bread.
— Health food store owner

I lost two hundred pounds of ugly fat; I divorced my husband.
— Smiling Ex-wife

On a flight from New Orleans to New York a few years ago, the pilot heard a strange sound. Throughout the plane could be heard a rhythmic thump, thump, thump. The pilot and the copilot checked and rechecked the instruments, the engineer looked around the plane, but the cause of the sound was not discovered.

They were about to turn back to New Orleans when the thumping stopped as suddenly and mysteriously as it had started. When the plane landed in New York, a stewardess came up to the pilot and said, "What a weird flight. This guy locked himself in the forward lavatory and jogged for twenty minutes."

Diet, exercise, be healthy . . . lose pounds while you sleep . . . run for your life . . . you are what you eat. Mark Twain said, "Be careful about reading health books. You might die of a misprint." A big business today, personal health care has benefited from scientific studies. For example, doctors have found that jogging releases endorphins, commonly known as the body's natural opiates or painkillers, into the bloodstream. Other doctors have discovered that laughter also produces the endorphins. Apparently, if you stand there and laugh at a jogger running by, you get the same effect.

About two years ago, a couple of entrepreneurs who met at a Jane Fonda workout class came up with the idea of a fleet of high-tech mobile fitness centers. Three times a week, a seventeen-foot luxury van equipped with $10,000 worth of exercise machinery — including everything from aerobics to biofeedback — would come to your home, office or studio by appointment. The drive-up concept was (at the time of the article) already franchised in forty-two cities. Unfortunately, that system wouldn't work for anyone whose office was in a two-story building with no elevator. They would have to *walk* down to the van.

Weight training for men has never been popular, except with a small segment of muscle-bound addicts. Now, women have discovered it as a means of "shaping" the body and have made it more popular than ever. A recent advertisement pitched "sculpturing" the body:

> Weight training isn't just for men — not anymore. All over the country women are using this sensible method to shape — literally sculpt — their bodies. Here, at last, is a fast, efficient way to burn fat, shape the body, firm up muscles and build stamina — all with no loss to your femininity. Yes, it may take just a few short weeks for you to feel better *all over* and look better *in all the right spots*, too.
> Includes: how to use fashion to camouflage those "chunky spots" until the new shape comes.

The advertisement also offered a money-back (or fat-back?) guarantee. The next thing *obliviosus* will come up with will be the Lizzie Borden Trim-Away-Those-Chunky-Spots Method: We pick you up and hack you off. Don't forget to wear your leg-warmers and Jockey panties.

* * *

Sociological Face-saving Note For Failed Dieters:

Fat people are more law-abiding. You never see a fat bank robber waddling away from the scene of the crime.

– 9 –

They Are Coming
to Get Us

*Don't look back. Something might be gaining on
you.*
— Leroy "Satchel" Paige

Sir Arthur Conan Doyle of Sherlock Holmes fame once sent a
telegram to each of twelve friends, all of whom were noted for
their virtue. The message said: "FLEE AT ONCE, ALL IS
DISCOVERED." Within twenty-four hours, all twelve had left
the country.

Just because you're not paranoid doesn't mean They are not
going to get you. Who are They? No one knows for sure (except
Them), but They have been conspiring against *obliviosus* since
the beginning of history. A sinister group, They have been known
as Lucifer, Pythagorian Cults, Gnostic Heretics, Knights Tem-
plar, Rosicrucians, Freemasons, Zionists, Jesuits, Communists,
International Bankers, and Illuminati. Everyone *knows* that J.F.K.
was assassinated by a Cuban-Mafia-KGB-CIA-FBI-LBJ-Howard
Hughes-Military/Industrial cabal.

In *Architects of Fear: Conspiracy Theory and Paranoia in
American Politics*, George X. Johnson reports that Albert Rivera,

107

an alleged ex-Jesuit pamphleteer, claims that a giant computer in the Vatican contains the names of all Protestants in preparation for a modern-day Inquisition. Members of the "Your Heritage Protection Association" claim that the Rothschilds assassinated President Lincoln.

A businesswoman from Alabama, Mary Stewart Relfe, in her 1981 fundamentalist best-seller, *When Your Money Fails — The "666" System is Here*, claimed that electronic banking and zebra-striped product codes are instruments of the devil and harbingers of the Apocalypse. In 1983, President Ronald Reagan told the National Association of Evangelicals that Communism is the "focus of evil in the modern world."

They are everywhere. Not only are They involved in grand conspiratorial schemes, They show Their hand in seemingly innocent, everyday events. In *The Conspiracy Against Childhood*, Eda J. LeShan reports a mimeographed notice sent to a fourteen-year-old schoolgirl for an overdue library book:

> If the book is not returned, we must make a notation of this on the PERMANENT RECORD CARD and we shall not be able to send any favorable recommendation for your daughter to any future business employer when she applies for a CIVIL SERVICE job, or when she applies to a business school or college.

LeShan comments that "somehow it seemed a little early to wipe out her entire future because of a lost book."

Thomas Pynchon, in *Gravity's Rainbow*, says that paranoia "is nothing less than the onset, the leading edge, of the discovery that *everything is connected*." Mark Richard Siegel, in *Pynchon:*

Creative Paranoia in Gravity's Rainbow, his exegesis of the work, says that "in both fiction-making and life, some sense of structure must be imposed on reality in order for human minds to grasp experience and to respond to it."

Siegel continues, "Some sort of paranoia, an oversensitivity to patterns, is necessary for the investigation of reality; They are not going to reveal Themselves when it is not to Their advantage to do so, and we must be constantly alert to the possibility of Their presence." The alternative to this paranoia, as Pynchon himself says in *Gravity's Rainbow*, is anti-paranoia, "where nothing is connected to anything, a condition not many of us can bear for long."

Since we know They are out there, what can we do to protect ourselves? One way, at least in a physical sense, to keep Them away from your door has been offered by *Grr-r-records*, a company in San Francisco. "Sebastian Speaks" is a thirty-six-minute recording of a German Shepherd barking and growling at spasmodic intervals. Available in LP and loop cassette, it can be played while you're out to keep Them away.

> *Does the name Pavlov ring a bell?*
> — Graffiti

We have observed *obliviosus* in efforts at self-expression, self-absorption and self-discovery. The efforts must have been debilitating, for now we find *obliviosus* in a state of self-surrender or helplessness. Not by choice, of course. They are doing it through what B.F. Skinner calls "operant conditioning," a form of behavior modification or reinforcement. Don't believe it? Fine. They don't want you to.

In *Science and Human Behavior*, Skinner reported a little trick that used to be employed to relieve boredom on sailing ships in the old days. The crew would take four or five cabin boys and fasten their hands to a ring around the mast. Then they gave each one a stick. All each boy had to do was to hit the boy ahead of him when he was hit from behind. It was in every boy's interest to hit lightly, but the hit you feel seems always a little harder than the one you give. In no time at all, quite predictably, the boys would be violently lashing at one another.

Well, you scoff, that's just normal behavior. No one can make you do anything you don't want to do, no matter how hard They try, right? In 1959, Aldous Huxley said: "Within the next generation or so people will have their liberties taken away from them, but will rather enjoy it because they will be distracted from any desire to rebel by propaganda . . . or brainwashing."

Earlier we used twenty-five years as a measure of one generation. Adding twenty-five years to 1959 brings us to 1984. These excerpts from reports which appeared in 1983 will serve as mileposts on the road to helplessness:

> Next time you hear music in the supermarket, listen carefully. Somebody may be trying to tell you something. A New Orleans firm with the foreboding name of Behavioral Engineering Corporation produces and leases recordings encoded with subliminal messages. One tape, leased to supermarkets, has a male voice that repeats phrases like "I am honest" and "We are a team." The tapes are designed to improve employee attitudes and discourage theft. One supermarket chain saw its loss due to damage and theft drop [and] six of fourteen stock boys quit after the tapes were installed.

> There is a danger that someone might use subliminals to manipulate large groups of people through radio or television. Unlikely, though, because it would

have to be done secretly, and too many people would be involved for the secret to keep for long."
— *San Diego Union,*
March 31, 1983

Before his death in 1980, psychiatrist and master hypnotist Milton Erickson had spent more than a half-century developing his own style of hypnosis, called "indirect induction." A properly trained practitioner could influence a subject's behavior by matching his verbal imagery, posture and rate of breathing; by "leading" or prompting slight changes in conduct through variations in language, voice and gesture; by "reframing" or offering suggestions that may shift a person's focus of attention; and by "anchoring," or linking key suggestions to specific sensations or perceptions such as a subtle touch or an approving wink. All these can be used to influence both conversation and thought.

[This] could be the most important synthesis of knowledge about human communication to emerge since the explosion of humanistic psychology in the sixties. At the moment, however, the task is to ensure that the patterns of covert communication do not become weapons in the hands of a new power elite.
— Flo Conway and Jim Siegelman,
The Awesome Power of the Mind Probers

According to these reports, Huxley may not have been too far off the mark. Since 1957, when a Fort Lee, New Jersey, movie theater flashed "Eat Popcorn" and "Drink Coca-Cola" messages for one-thousandth of a second during the film, *obliviosus* had progressed to 1984, when supermarket shoppers returned home wondering why they had purchased thirty dollars worth of non-food items and three cases of succotash.

Of course, the methods used today are not called
                                    YOU
"propaganda" or "brainwashing." The key word now is
                                    WILL
"subliminal," defined as any image, word or sound that
                                    TELL
is perceived outside the "normal" range of consciousness,
                                    ALL
but which nevertheless makes an impression in the mind.
                                    OF
This can mean words or pictures flashed so fast we can't
                                    YOUR
recall seeing them or words hidden in the background of
                                    FRIENDS
sound, evoking no conscious memory. It can also mean
                                    TO
images in print advertisements that do not move, but are
                                    BUY
"buried" or "incorporated" into the artwork, conveying
                                    THIS
their messages to the subconscious. All of this is
                                    BOOK
rather new. In ancient times, behavior modifcation was
                                    (WINK)
called "slavery," not as subtle, but effective nevertheless.

> *A phony press release is known as "artificial*
> *dissemination."*
> — BL

Is *obliviosus* getting the complete story? Are They keeping
something hidden? Who *are* They, anyway? Are They in control
of the media? Do They start all the unfounded rumors? Who has
the answers? Who's asking the questions?

In antiquity, the poet Vergil noted: *fama volat* (rumor flies). More recently, Norman Mailer gave the name "factoid" to tales which, though unfounded, appear in the press and are repeated afterwards as facts. The tales, stories, or "news items," as they are euphemistically called by the media, are not always events of major significance, but a small lie is a lie, the same as The Big Lie. The Big Lie affects more people in a more instantaneous way, such as *The War of the Worlds* broadcast by Orson Welles in 1938. The small lie grows through rumor, and quickly spreads among the populace.

Sometimes the small lie is humorous, with no apparent harm done. One such "news item" has been around a long time and is occasionally resurrected by a bored newsperson manning the graveyard shift at a city desk:

Last night a Dumbville resident was reminded of the importance of communicating ideas in an unambiguous manner. A man's car was stalled on the side of the road. He flagged down another car for help.

"I need a push," he told the driver of the assisting car, "but this has an automatic transmission, so we'll have to get it up to thirty-five miles an hour before it'll start."

"OK," said the driver, who began backing the car into position.

The man got into his stalled car, turned on the ignition key and waited — and waited. Wondering what was taking so long, he looked into his rearview mirror to see the other car coming . . . at thirty-five miles an hour!

In *The World Is Coming to an End*, Victor Hicken quotes

Samuel Beers of Harvard in a 1979 *National Observer* editorial: "The media revolution is as powerful as the industrial revolution was. The word manipulators are on top. My students leave here and go into journalism and wield enormous power."

In a note to that comment, Hicken adds that "any deep investigation of television corporate holdings would also indicate an enormous financial power as well." Dale Minor, in *The Information War*, gives the example of RCA, which bought NBC in 1926 and later purchased Random House — which had previously bought Alfred A. Knopf. CBS was the parent company to Holt, Rinehart and Winston, while ABC merged with ITT in 1967. Yes, and all of it is owned by the Howard Hughes estate, Yoko Ono, executor.

* * *

A man related the story of how, as a young boy, he became aware of an insidious fear of Them. Awakening from a fitful sleep in his darkened bedroom, he felt something caught between his toes. A little concentration and a few toe movements proved it was not the sheet. Half-asleep but curious, he sat up in bed and reached down to feel the thing that was tickling his feet. It seemed to be stuck, so he pulled it. It came away in his hand with an ominous ripping sound. Now curiosity had turned to anxiety, and the boy padded into the bathroom, turned on the light, and read the words printed on the small rectangular cloth: DO NOT REMOVE UNDER PENALTY OF LAW.

The boy turned off the light, crept back to bed, stuffed the tag under his pillow, and lay awake staring at the door, waiting for Them to come and get him.

– 10 –
I Think, Therefore
I Am a Computer

Progress might have been alright once but it has gone on too long.

— Ogden Nash

Almost five hundred passengers were in their seats as the inaugural journey of the California Bullet Train got underway. As the train left San Francisco and began speeding its way through tunnels and over bridges along the San Andreas fault, an assuring voice came over the loudspeaker system:

Ladies and gentlemen, there is no crew on this train, but there is nothing to worry about. This entire system is fully computerized and automated, representing the latest developments in modern technology. You will be transported to Southern California at speeds in excess of two hundred miles per hour in perfect safety. Every operation has been tested and retested. There is not the slightest chance that anything can go wrong . . . go wrong . . . go wrong . . .

Regardless of what has been said about "Mad Scientists," science itself is not bad. Where *obliviosus* goes off on tangents is

115

in the area of science applied in a practical manner, sometimes laughingly known as technology.

Inventions are often anachronistic. As we have seen, the wheel was invented long before the brake. Another example of mistiming, in this case for the better, is that the bathtub was invented in 1850 and the telephone in 1875. If you had been living in 1850, you could have sat in the tub for twenty-five years without the phone's ringing once.

Since then, not much has developed in the way of bathtubs except for adding little motorized currents and calling them Whirlpools or Jacuzzis, but the telephone industry developed into one of the largest corporations in the world, only to be disassembled into a number of counterproductive elements, all of which are computerized to the hilt.

A result of this application of modern technology to what used to be "Listen, Harry — two rings, there's another call for Mildred" on the old party-line system can be seen in the case of the Automatic-Dialing Telephone Sales Computer in Los Angeles calling New York City on a Friday night and getting a call-forwarding to an answering machine with an intercept from the phone company saying "Sorry, your call did not go through. Please hang up and dial again." By the time all of the machines were discovered still talking to one another on Monday morning, a $5,000 phone bill had been rung up.

Technology covers a wide range of history and a wide variety of applications. In *The Living Past,* Lissner relates this technological anecdote:

> A chance stroke of good fortune has preserved for us [the imprint of] a dainty little shoe which, 2,400 years ago, belonged to a Greek streetwalker. Nailed onto the sole of this shoe are the words "Follow Me" set in such a manner that this pert invitation was

imprinted in the soft dirt of the streets as the girl strolled along.

While the application of several sciences are at work in Lissner's example, science and technology have not always served *obliviosus* well. In *The Concise Encyclopedia of Ancient Civilizations,* edited by Janet Serlin Garber, it is reported that the Sung Dynasty of China, which lasted for over three hundred years (A.D. 960-1279), was a period of political experimentation and brilliant cultural accomplishments.

Some of the Sung innovations were as modern as anything reported in today's newspaper. They had a national budget, unemployment tax, graduated income tax, low-interest loans for farmers (well, maybe not today's paper), price and commodity control, paper money, and enforced military service. The compass was applied to navigation, movable type was invented, and gunpowder was used for warfare.

The three-hundred-year-old, technology-rich Sung Dynasty had its cultural clock cleaned by a mob of barbarian Mongols led by Genghis Khan who overran them and conquered all of China in less than five years.

> *How do you explain "counterclockwise" to some-*
> *one with a digital watch?*
>
> — BL

A look at some of the current applications of science will show that *obliviosus* is certain that today we are living in the best of all possible worlds. John D. MacDonald, through his hero Travis McGee, says: "I always buy beer in cans with the pull tàbs. You stare at the tab, think deep thoughts about progress, modern living, cultural advances; and then you turn the can upside down and open it with a can opener. It is a ceremonial kind of freedom."

Pull tabs, or the later "lift and punch a hole in the can" tabs are a great technological advance. The idea of the "lift and punch" type is to avoid the discarding of the pull tab, an improvement which supposedly cuts down tremendously on the litter problem. However, even with the self-contained type, you have to twist the tab off or you may get an unplanned and unprofessional nose job. If you do twist it off, more than likely it will fall into the can. It is about the right size, if swallowed, to engrave The Lord's Prayer on your intestinal tract.

Another great feat of today's technology is the package. An almost indestructible nine-volt battery for a transistor radio is hermetically sealed in a plastic bubble-pack that takes three eight-year-old kids and a grownup fifteen minutes to open. A loaf of bread, or anything fragile that you plan to feed your family and hope that it is fresh and sanitary, is thrown into a bag of .00001-gauge plastic and twisted with a little piece of wire covered with paper to hide the rust.

Obliviosus is presently working on innovations such as freeze-dried grits, gas-operated television sets, and computer-controlled automobiles. That last bears some speculation; you could computerize all of the cars on the road today, and one of them would still pull out to pass.

Raymond Chandler, in *The Long Goodbye,* commented on the phenomenon of technological quality:

> You can't expect quality from people whose lives
> are a subjection to a lack of quality. You can't have
> quality with mass production. You don't want it
> because it lasts too long. So you substitute styling,
> which is a commercial swindle intended to produce

artificial obsolescence. Mass production couldn't sell
its goods next year unless it made what it sold this year
look unfashionable a year from now.

We have the whitest kitchens and the most shining
bathrooms in the world. But in the lovely white
kitchen the average American housewife can't produce
a meal fit to eat, and the lovely shining bathroom is
mostly a receptacle for deodorants, laxatives, sleeping
pills, and the products of that confidence racket called
the cosmetic industry. We make the finest packages in
the world, Mr. Marlowe. The stuff inside is mostly
junk.

*Sticks and stones may break my bones, But whips
and chains excite me.*

— Graffiti

No matter what the quality, things still have to be made, and
someone has to do the work of making them. After suffering from
self-surrender, or helplessness, *obliviosus* has now arrived at the
epitome of knowledge: the ability to delegate work, which has the
ultimate consequence of delegating responsibility.

A time-tested way to delegate work is through the use of
slavery. Whether it be people, automatons, machines or computers, the principle of automatic work — morality aside — is the
same. Mass production is a lot of the same things made
repetitiously by a few people. The antithesis of mass production
is a lot of repetitious people working on the same thing, such as
the building of an Egyptian pyramid or the World Trade Center.

The word *slave* comes from eighth-century France where
princes and bishops were blessed with a plethora of Slavonian
bondsmen. But no society in history, before or since, has been

119

able to devise a way of life without some form of slavery. Roman slaves from Gaul were exhibited for purchasers with a label attached to the neck of each. The estimated age of the individual, country of origin, and qualities or defects were noted on the label. Second-hand slaves were of less value, as they were likely to be idle and cunning. If representations on the label later proved to be false, the buyer could sue. If the slave was sold without a warranty, he or she was exhibited with a cap on the head.

While "used" slaves were often idle and cunning, "new" slaves sometimes did not understand — or accept — their role. In *The Long Road West,* Frank Morley tells of the experience of the Spanish slave-owners in Hispaniola:

> In the beginning of the 16th century, the Indians of the New World were given the title "Freemen" by the Spaniards, and it was to be understood that they had exactly the same rights and privileges as the legally-free peasants of Spain. Unfortunately (for the Spaniards), there was a terminology gap, because when the Indians heard they were free men, they ran off into the bush. Within a few months, the settlements were without food or water. There was no solution except to round up the Indians and teach them to be Spanish peasants.

Throughout history, it was continually evident that human slavery would always be subject to inefficiency and rebellion. In some cases, even guilt — for why else would there be a desire to "set free" the more "human" slaves? The answer to these problems has repeated itself ever since the creation myths: *obliviosus* could make or "create" another creature to assist him. Attempts have been made at recreating humans in the forms of Homunculi, Golems, Pygmalions and Frankenstein monsters. The reverse desire to make some humans into statues has also been expressed in the stories of Medusa, Lot's wife, and civil service workers.

Monsters, however, have a history of going berserk. In Mary Shelley's *Frankenstein,* the monster was not created evil and is depicted as an intelligent, opinionated, loquacious creature with a Hamletian mentality who goes wrong only when he becomes disillusioned by the "misery, vice, bloodshed and hatred" that he discovers while among the "real people" of the world. This theme proved too subtle for Hollywood, and the monster in the movie was given a criminal brain, a dose of lightning, and the resulting mentality of a flashlight battery.

> *Please remain seated until your elephant comes to a full stop.*
>
> — Sign at Disneyland

Having failed at creating another human being, *obliviosus* turned to mechanical devices, automatons and androids. A man named Maetzel once invented a robot that could play chess. Some thought there was a man inside. There was. In the movie *Star Wars,* two of the main characters were the robots R2-D2 and C-3PO. Some thought there were men inside. There were, although most overlooked that and personified the machines. Today, computerized robots contain no hidden humans but are doing so much thinking that the mental evolution of *obliviosus* may be destined to dependency on the machines.

This evolutionary stage is recent, but the automatons have been around since (and probably before, if you count Trojan Horses, etc.) Archytas of Tarentum, a friend of Plato's, made a wooden pigeon that could fly. In the thirteenth century, Albertus Magnus — although it may have been partly myth — built a doorkeeper to stand outside his room in the monastery. It was built of wax, metal, leather and wood and was said to have greeted visitors, asked their business, and engaged in pleasantries until the bishop could answer the call in person. Today, it would receive a dozen roses during National Secretaries Week. According to the legend, one of Albertus's pupils, Thomas Aquinas, became so annoyed with the android that he took a club to it one day.

René Descartes was said to have constructed a female android named Francine. In 1637 Descartes wrote that mankind would someday construct "soulless machinery" that would behave like animals. Not only was that statement prophetic, but it makes one wonder what kind of an animal Francine behaved like.

About a hundred years after Descartes, another Frenchman, an engineer named Jacques deVaucanson, created several automatons and androids. One of his automatons was a mechanical duck with a thousand moving parts. It could "eat" and "digest" food. The poet Goethe saw the duck years later and wrote an entry in his diary: "The duck was like a skeleton and had digestive problems."

Of course, machines — even when computerized — can go berserk, the same as slaves or monsters. One short circuit, and a mechanical arm on an assembly line that is supposed to cap bottles will instead hit more home runs than Babe Ruth, Roger Maris, Mickey Mantle and Hank Aaron all put together.

At the 1939 World's Fair in New York, one feature was a walking robot named Electro and his robot dog, Sparko. Electro talked to the crowds, and Sparko barked and begged. About forty years later, robot expert Hans Moravec, of Carnegie-Mellon University of Pittsburgh, created Rover, a robot-dog that judges the state of the environment around him and considers his best interests. If the dog spots an obstacle in its path, it stops to examine it before it goes on its way.

If this is a trend in creating dogs, *obliviosus* will have to come up with a new, improved idea in mechanical rovers. One suggestion is to create a dog on the thinking order of R2-D2, which could be named SN9K9. A prototype of this model (subsequently named 2BZ2P) has been developed but needs some modification, as it continues to destroy itself by chasing parked cars.

> *I can tell from your voice harmonics, Dave, that you're badly upset. Why don't you take a stress pill and get some rest?*
>
> — HAL, the computer in
> *2001: A Space Odyssey*

Automatons, robots and androids are fun, but the real concern of computer technology is the business of intelligence, and the growing field of artificial intelligence is seeking not so much to replicate the human brain as to utilize the capabilities of computers to enhance the human mind.

In doing so, however, the computer is laying waste to many inefficient human thinkers who can no longer "trick' their way into usefulness. Over the long run, computerized technology will increase unemployment. Professor Nils Nilsson, director of the Stanford Research Institute's Artificial Intelligence Lab, has said, "There are a lot of dumb jobs out there that should be eliminated." A recent newspaper item states that, by 1990, half of the work force in the United States is expected to know how to use computers. The other half will be computers. The *Harvard Business Review* recently said that, at present, one robot does the work of up to six people, and new, more sophisticated robots coming along will displace as many as 3.8 million workers.

But unemployment is not as large a specter as is the possibility of the human brain's being not replicated, but replaced by the computer. Not all human brains, of course; They are still there. But some indications of this are already in evidence. To see the effect of computers on the human brain, simply go into any store, purchase something, and give the clerk an odd amount of money.

For example, if the amount is $2.96, give three one-dollar bills, two dimes and a penny. You have a logical desire to obtain one quarter with which you may buy a newspaper from an uncomputerized vending machine, rather than ending up with two dimes and five pennies. Watch the clerk closely. If the cash register is computerized, the amount tendered will be entered and the correct change — twenty-five cents — will be displayed. If the register is not computerized or if the clerk has not learned to trust the computerized register yet, watch as the clerk develops a mental hernia trying to understand the transaction.

Putting the average human brain on the edge of a razor blade is like rolling a BB down the center of an eight-lane highway.

— BL

Replacement of the human brain by computers is not the only concern of *obliviosus*. Computer scientists are presently experimenting with "chemical" computers — computers "grown" by bacteria spiked with artificial computer genes. Also in the experimental stage, but becoming rapidly more advanced, is the coupling, or "interfacing," of the brain directly with a computer (as shown in the movie *Brainstorm*). A brain coupled to a computer would not have to use memory or reason on its own. Just "plug in" and automatically one would be able to speak Mandarin Chinese or make change in odd amounts with no problems.

Douglas R. Hofstadter, in his book *Godel, Escher, Bach: An Eternal Golden Braid,* says that people are being asked to view computers as "our partners in evolution. Not enough people," he continues, "are saying, wait a minute, how do we really think, what is consciousness, and where does our sense of self come from?"

Could a mob of barbarians overrun our technology-rich society the way the Mongols did China a thousand years ago? Ivar Lissner, in the closing comment to his book, *The Living Past,* provides, if not the answer, at least a climactic statement:

> Whether we of today, with our "exact sciences," are pursuing more perilous chimeras than the ancient world did remains to be seen. The only certainty is that if the intellectual development of the West continues lagging, as it has, behind our indisputably great scientific achievements, we shall one day be like small children playing with large and dangerous toys which they do not understand, or will become specialist technicians pressing buttons and unleashing forces whose moral implications we are no longer capable of assessing.

* * *

A recent newspaper item reported that Lloyd Stallkamp, a teacher of electronics at National College in Rapid City, South Dakota, took issue with Albert Einstein's theory that light is composed of tiny particles called "photons." He announced his discovery that dark is composed of tiny particles called "darkons."

Stallkamp said he doesn't know the speed of dark, "but it must be faster than light."

Part Three

—●—

Power

May the Force be with you.

— Obi-Wan Kenobi

Obedience, Outrage
and Oblivion

At a meeting in an Iron Curtain country, one of the Party members, Comrade Dobrinsky, got up and said, "Comrade Leader, I have only three questions to ask. If we are the greatest industrial nation in the world, what happened to our automobiles? If we have the best agriculture in the world, what happened to our bread? If we are the finest cattle raisers in the world, what happened to our meat?"

The Party chairman stared at Comrade Dobrinsky for a few long moments, then spoke: "It is too late to reply to your questions tonight. I will answer them fully at our next meeting."

When the meeting opened the following week, another Party member rose and said, "I have just one question. What happened to Comrade Dobrinsky?"

The greatest threat to power is a challenge to that power. It is a utilitarian fact that in every complicated society there has to be someone to do the dirty work. As long as there are obedient people, there is no problem. A problem arises when the ones who rule the obedient ones begin to think that they are better in some essential way than their subservient counterparts. They may, in fact, be in a better position, but they are as oblivious as the next guy and encounter age-old difficulties when they begin to use their power to do what they think is best for everyone else.

Outrageous acts of power escalate into contests, inviting challenge. The ghostly battle cries of the ages never cease to reverberate in the sea of time; the tears for fallen sons and lovers hardly cease before they begin again.

There are approximately sixty thousand nuclear bombs throughout the world, with ten new ones being made every day. There are over four tons of explosive power available for every man, woman and child in the world. *Obliviosus* courts oblivion.

– 11 –

To You, It's Genocide;
To Me, It's Manifest Destiny

*Why would we have different races if God meant us
to be alike and associate with one another?*
— Lester Maddox

A tourist traveling through the Southwest bought a silver and turquoise bracelet from an Indian for ten dollars. The Indian assured the traveler that it was authentic tribal craftsmanship. He told how his squaw had learned the art from her great-grandmother.

An hour later, the tourist returned red-faced with anger, shouting "There's a fellow on the other side of town selling these same things for five dollars! This shows you can't trust an Indian!"

"No," replied the Indian, unperturbed. "It shows you can't trust a white man. The guy who sold me this stuff told me I had an exclusive for this town."

The word *barbarian* comes from the Greek expression ridiculing anyone who didn't speak the Greek language. All other languages, to them, sounded like the "bar-bar" ("bah-bah" we would say) noise that sheep make (a kind of "It's Greek to me" in reverse). Except for some movies and pulp literature, the word *barbarian* is not in wide use today. It has been replaced by a number of shorter epithets, and every group has a stinging one for

131

every other group.

Gordon W. Allport, a Professor of Social Ethics at Harvard University, published a pamphlet entitled *ABC's of Scapegoating*, in which he lists the four stages of hostile behavior between groups. *Predilection*, the first, is a simple preference for one culture, color or language as opposed to another: You like Mexican food; I don't. I'll order something else. *Prejudice*, the second stage, is a closed-minded attitude of prejudgment, impervious to evidence: All women are inferior to men. "Prejudice," Allport says, "if not *acted out*, does no great *social* harm. It merely stultifies the mind that possesses it." But prejudice expressed leads to *Discrimination*, the third stage, an act of exclusion prompted by a prejudice: Women cannot belong to a men's club, but Mexican food may be served there.

The final stage of hostile behavior is *Scapegoating*, which is full-fledged aggression in word or deed. Allport defines scapegoating as "a phenomenon wherein some of the aggressive energies of a person or a group are focused upon another individual, group, or object; the amount of aggression and blame being either partly or wholly unwarranted."

In scapegoating, Allport continues, "the victim is abused verbally or physically. He usually cannot fight back, for we see to it that we pick only on minority groups weaker than ourselves." Besides women and Mexican food, some of history's favorite scapegoats have included Jews, Negroes, Scotsmen, Irishmen, Catholics, American Indians, and even the Salem "witches," a group of children and frail old ladies who could not offer effective resistance. You wouldn't see a bigot walking up to Mr. T and calling him a son-of-a-witch.

One of the things that helps at least predilection along, if not some of the later stages, is humor. Most of the humor in the world makes fun of somebody. When the humor is directed at a specific group, it treads on ground littered with little warning signs identifying the four stages of hostile behavior.

For instance, there are those storytellers who feel they must use dialect to enhance their tale. If it is not essentially demeaning to an identifiable group, they may get away with it. The worst kind of storyteller is the one who begins, "I'm not good at dialect, but I'll try anyway." His story goes something like this: "Well, so Pat sez to Mike, 'Bejabbers me bye, und vy dun't you esking hahcum all dem dere lil chirren am sho nuff eading veener-vurst mit sowergraut befo dey go to da moom pitch in-a da beeg ceety?' " Anyone who tells a joke like that is usually wearing a plaid threepiece suit with a red tie, white belt and white shoes — or has an outfit like that in his closet.

Sometimes ethnic humor can be quaint (He would last as long in a national election as a paper shirt in a bear fight), clever (A country judge shooed away a fly. The farmer on trial says, "They like to land onto a horse's rear end." The judge asks if he is being compared to a horse's rear end. The farmer says, "I know the difference, but the fly doesn't"), or relatively harmless (In the South, children have names like "Butterfly" and "Truth"; in the Southwest, they have names like "Deer Crossing" and "Falling Rocks"). Of course, some jokes can be applied to any individual or group of your choice, for example, ridiculing a lack of intelligence or simplemindedness — Want to go out by the pool? It'll take about thirty minutes to blow it up.

Occasionally, humor can be directed at a helpless person in an unusual stituation and still remain funny because it is ultimately harmless. (Remember the blind man looking around in the department store by swinging his seeing-eye dog in circles over his head?) Here's an example based on a factual newspaper item:

In Houston, a man who stole his father's wooden legs and held them for ransom has been sentenced to

133

ten years' probation on burglary charges. Calvin Joseph, 27, admitted to police that he stole the wooden legs of his father, Percy Joseph, 54, and ordered the older man to feed him or else he would not return the devices [the unusual situation].

[And here comes the joke.] A suit for $1 million in damages filed against the son by the father was thrown out of court. The judge said the father didn't have a leg to stand on.

[It is] our Manifest Destiny to overspread the continent allotted by Providence for the free development of our yearly multiplying millions.
  — 1845 editorial by John L.O'Sullivan
    (first usage of the phrase which became the catchword for American expansionism)

Noticing differences becomes much more serious when actions toward a particular group pass through prejudice, beyond scapegoating, and develop into genocidal activities. A superior attitude demands obedience, and genocide is the ultimate method of behavior control. Throughout the history of *obliviosus*, the idea of racial superiority has had dire consequences.

Genocide has a way of starting with innuendo and ending with the rampant destruction of human lives. Twenty-six million Chinese killed during Mao Tse-Tung's regime between 1949 and 1965; ten million farmers killed during the Russian Great Purge of 1936-1938; six million Jews killed in the Holocaust surrounding World War II; three million Cambodians killed during the Pol Pot rule between 1975 and 1979. Politics, crusades, slavery, massacres, inquisitions — *obliviosus* has continually assisted nature's plagues and cataclysms in the effort toward population control.

The following quotation is offered with a blank in the place of the name of a particular group of people. Except for some clues innate in the item, you may add the name of whatever racial group suits your predilection:

> There never was a full-blooded _____ who took to civilization. It was not in their nature. He believed they were destined to extinction, and although he would never use or countenance inhumanity toward them, he did not think them, as a race, worth preserving. He considered them as essentially inferior to the Anglo-Saxon race, which were now taking their place on this continent. They were not an improvable breed, and their disappearance from the human family will be no great loss to the world. In point of fact they were rapidly disappearing, and he did not believe that in fifty years from this time there would be any of them left.

Fill in the blank with *Indian*. The comment was the view of Henry Clay, U.S. Secretary of State, as paraphrased by John Quincy Adams in his dairy of 1825. The American Indian is a perfect example of what happens when you "let" the government take care of you.

Notice the use of "they," "their" and "them." It is distracting to the purposes of prejudice to consider a single person rather than a group. It makes the scapegoating activities seem more "personal." A look at American Indians in general, the "noble savages" "inferior to the Anglo-Saxon race," can be made somewhat less disdainful if one particular individual is observed.

Who among us has not used the memory of past events to help in recalling dates? The following excerpt from James H. Breasted's *The Conquest of Civilization*, in contrast to Clay's view, is a look at just one Indian:

Lone Dog, a Dakota chief, had a buffalo robe with seventy-one named years recorded on it, beginning in 1800, when he was a child of four. A year when whooping-cough was very bad was called the Whooping-Cough Year; its sign shows a human head coughing violently. Another year, very plentiful in meteors, was called the Meteor Year, and its sign was a rude drawing of a falling meteor. A third year saw the arrangement of peace between the Dakotas and the Crows; its sign was therefore two Indians, with differing style of hair indicating the two different tribes, exchanging pipes of peace.

Thus, instead of saying, as we do, that a thing happened in the year 1813, the Indian said it happened in the Whooping-Cough Year, and by examining his table of years could tell how far back that year was.

Allport says that the scale of behavior between groups (and individuals, as well) can move in the other direction from predilection. Instead of toward hostility, behavior can move toward friendliness through the stages of tolerance, respect and cooperation. While this has occasionally been effected through legal means, the main hinderance seems to be that it is not in the nature of *obliviosus* to remember that any progress has ever been made.

* * *

A Japanese businessman, wearing a suit tailored in Hong Kong and traveling on a Russian airliner, landed in the American city of Anchorage, Alaska. Lighting his English cigarette with a German cigarette lighter, he looked at his Swiss watch, then walked into the gift shop at the airport. He purchased an Eskimo souvenir made in Taiwan to send to his Swedish wife who was visiting her parents in South Africa.

An American businessman, also browsing in the gift shop, spotted the Japanese man and mumbled something to his companion about how the Japs ought to keep their cars in their own country, where they belong.

– 12 –

You Can't Put a Barbed-Wire Fence Across the Mississippi

I don't feel we did wrong in taking this great country away from them. There were great numbers of people who needed land, and the Indians were selfishly trying to keep it for themselves.

— John Wayne

According to the *Journal of Irreproducible Results*, a geographer noted that the major landmasses and peninsulas point south — Africa, South America, Florida, Baja California, Malaya, India, Greece, Italy, Spain, etc. The land appears to have been poured onto the earth from the North Pole and run down over the globe like the paint in the old Sherwin-Williams "We Cover the Earth" logo. This is known as the Theory of Continental Drip.

Land is something you graze on, dig into, rent out, or fight over. In ancient times, the cultivators of land worked on property owned by the tribe. Eventually, private ownership by families came to be recognized, which led to disputes about boundaries, inheritances, and other legal business that required an authority. Settling disputes tended to create a government, which is to be expected when bad comes to worse.

Another look at Lo, the Poor Indian, will serve to illustrate one government's method of settling disputes. In this case, Lo's name is Osceola, the leader of the Seminoles of Florida. When Andrew Jackson had a "removal" program to clean the Indians out of Florida, the Seminoles, led by Osceola, defied an army sent to effect a forced removal.

The war lasted seven years and cost the lives of fifteen hundred troops and an expenditure of $40 million. Osceola hid the women and children in the great Florida swamps and fought a skillful guerilla war. The United States Army triumphed, however. Osceola was captured when he trusted a flag of truce in going to a peace conference and was imprisoned until his death. Evidently, Henry Clay was right when he said it was not in the Indian's nature to take to civilization. Imagine trusting a flag of truce — how primitively naive!

I will find the way or make one.

— Hannibal

Obliviosus has made maps of the known world since before Homer's time. As soon as explorers discovered a new place, cartographers drew it on a map, politicians claimed it, and soldiers went out to get it. The fact that someone might already be there did not deter them in the least. Alexander the Great thought he had conquered the whole world, but he didn't even get as far as New Jersey.

Once a location is defined on a map it can be given a name, but you have to go there and occupy it before it becomes a territory. Robert Ardrey, in *The Territorial Imperative*, points out that a territory is particularly important to male members of most species of animals: the female of the species will have nothing to do with a male who does not "own" a little property.

Ardrey also notes that "in most, but not all territorial species, defense is directed only against fellow members of the kind. A squirrel does not regard a mouse as a trespasser." This explains why the Trojan Horse worked and suggests that an army of squirrels could march on Moscow without a shot being fired.

Sometimes it is difficult to enforce territorial boundaries. In *The Lure of the Land*, Everett Dick tells of the loggers in 1860 "cutting a round forty." Having rights to cut forty acres in the midst of public lands, the boss would send his crew to log "around the forty acres." The crew would cut the timber in the forty acres, then in the forty acres to the north, and to the south, east and west, for a total of two hundred acres.

Another method was "throwing the chain," which involved, according to Dick, "the simple operation of moving a section line a few rods east, west, north or south of the true line and by this maneuver making a quarter section or even a forty include an exceptionally fine streak of pine lying just beyond the true line. When a logger was caught at this, it was explained as a topographical error."

One of the things landowners throughout history have had to enforce their territorial boundaries against is the avid hunter. Hunters have been known to shoot up anything that moves and many shiny or brightly colored things that do not. On occasion, a human is mistaken for a deer, a bear or a moose and done in by an eager hunter. Anyone who is mistaken for a moose and shot is better off dead, anyway.

Hunters are not too perceptive when it comes to distinguishing varieties of animals. One farmer ran across a hunter in his field, and the hunter tried to make conversation: "Oh, what a funny-looking cow. But why doesn't it have horns?" The farmer replied: "There are many reasons why a cow does not have horns. Some grow horns late in life. Others have been dehorned. Some breeds are not supposed to have horns. This cow does not have horns for another reason, however. It's a horse."

One landowner who continually had trouble keeping hunters

off his property decided to post NO TRESPASSING signs. No one paid attention to these, so he put up several NO HUNTING signs. Didn't work either. Getting serious, he put up several big signs saying STAY OFF OR GET SHOT. Overrun with hunters who not only ignored, but shot up all the signs he made, he finally thought of a sign that should — and did — work: COPPERHEAD SANCTUARY.

> *A verbal contract isn't worth the paper it's written on.*
>
> — Samuel Goldwyn

Land can be inherited, granted, or purchased. But that's only the small, legitimate part. There are other ways to acquire land, including warfare, which we will consider in detail later. Warfare has the unpleasant side effect of devastating much of the acquisition. Other methods of acquiring land range from mild deception to murder.

Some territorial struggles have been fought — and won — in the bedroom or the nursery (seven- or eight-year-old kids getting married for political or geographical reasons, for instance). The "weaker sex" of pre-liberation days also knew a thing or two about getting territory, as these examples show:

IRENE (A.D. 752-803): Byzantine Empress (after the Roman Empire) from A.D. 797-802. She married Leo IV, and he died ten years later. She ruled while her son was a minor, but in 790 she was removed from power. She schemed her way back and had her son's eyes stabbed out. She became sole ruler of Byzantium, the first woman to govern, but signed herself Emperor because of the strong prejudice against a woman ruler.

WU HU (A.D. 625-705): Empress of China from A.D. 690-705, only female sovereign of her nation; ruled during the T'ang Dynasty. She was taken into the emperor's harem at age twelve and retired to a nunnery at age twenty-four when a new emperor came along. She forced the new emperor to banish his wife by a series of intrigues. He then made her empress, and she dominated him until his death. She was arrogant, cruel and overbearing and called herself Empress God Almighty.

AGRIPPINA THE YOUNGER (A.D. 15-59): The sister of Caligula and Mother of Nero. Her brother Caligula exiled her when she was twenty-four, but two years later her uncle Claudius became emperor, recalled her, and married her. She persuaded him to choose Nero, her son by her first marriage, over his son as his heir. He did, then she poisoned her uncle/husband so Nero could become emperor. Nero returned the favor to his mother five years later by poisoning her.

(Isn't one of these girls on *Dynasty*?)

These examples, of course, transcend simple land deals and pass well beyond territory into the realm of kingdoms. Examples that ordinary, everyday *obliviosus* can relate to can be found in more recent times. In the nineteenth century, when the American government had run off most of the Indians, the squatters ran ahead of treaties, surveys, and land auctions in order to get the choice locations.

Some of these were called "sooners," as they would get out to a preferential site in advance of a land race, hide in a ditch or a bush, and jump out after the rush started, claiming the land before anyone else got to it, telling them they got there "sooner." A few vigilante-types got upset at this method, and arriving claimants found some men hanging from trees with a sign reading "Too Soon" pinned on their chests.

In *The Lure of the Land*, Everett Dick explains that the right to "pre-emption" required a family to "improve land for the purpose of making a home as a prerequisite for the right of buying the land at the minimum price." As a show of improvement was as important as prior occupancy, there were several methods of filling that requirement. Dick relates one effort, a legitimate attempt at improvement, which occurred during one of the great races for public land:

> The most common proof of improvement in this treeless country was to start digging a well or a cellar. Of course, a man could carry a spade on horseback while making a run for land. A young man and his sister at the starting line, mounted on horses and waiting to make the run, were excited and anxious, for they knew where they wanted to locate. "Now Betty," the brother said, "be sure to follow me and keep up with me if you can, for I have the spade to commence our improvements and I am going to ride on a dead run."
>
> But in the wild rush following the bark of the signal guns, the brother and sister were separated. When the young man reached the location he found that his sister had outrun him and, having no implement, was burrowing in the ground with her hands like a badger.

Some not-so-legitimate methods of improvement are also revealed in *The Lure of the Land*. Some of the stipulations of the law that proved settlement were: "Is it habitable?"; "Does it have a window?"; "Does it have a plank floor?"; "Is it twelve by fourteen?" According to Dick, "Some pre-emptors dropped a stone at each corner of an imaginary house, split a small stick and

144

ON EDGAR BERGEN'S LAP

inserted a piece of glass, then placed the 'window' on one side of the 'house.' A plank would be laid on the ground inside the 'house' and the sham homemaker would sleep on the plank one night. He could then swear that he had a habitable residence with a plank floor and a glass window." Some, he continues, had a little house whittled out with a pen knife, twelve by fourteen inches, so they could claim they had a house "twelve by fourteen." One Nebraska claimant had a small frame house built on a wagon and pulled it by oxen from claim to claim. It would stop at each claim for a day or two while witnesses came to view the "improvement."

Without getting into money or politics (coming up next), natural resources (coming later), or warfare (coming last), what *can* you do with land, anyway? Live on it. OK, but you don't live on all of it; you walk around on it, maybe, but you live on only a small part. You have to use it in some way.

Perhaps Attila or Alexander or Agrippina could rattle off the uses for all the varieties of land they controlled, but in order to make this analogy more understandable to the average *obliviosus*, let's say you have become the proud owner of a piece of land two inches square. Unless you're a very determined ballet dancer, you can't live on it, so that takes care of one option.

After a little thought, you decide that it is probably best to use it for agriculture as the mining, grazing or hydroelectric potentials seem rather insignificant. You decide that you will plant beans — or rather, bean. In order to protect the planting, you may have to build a fence, but that won't cost too much unless the fence is very tall. A fence too tall, however, would create a problem in harvesting the crop.

When the crop is in, you truck it to the market for sale, although you could work out a partnership with someone in the pork business. You are now a farmer. Next year, the government will pay you money not to grow bean.

145

* * *

The *Journal of Irreproducible Results* reports that the earth is heading for destruction in the near future. Projections indicate that the North American continent will be wrenched by massive earthquakes and landslides, with most of it sinking into the ocean. The cause of this catastrophe that will spell the end of land is the accumulated weight of back issues of *National Geographic* magazine.

– 13 –

John or Jane,
The Does are Always
Looking for a Fast Buck

I've been rich and I've been poor; rich is better.
— Sophie Tucker

In one of the well-to-do suburbs of Atlanta, a number of wealthy neighbors got together every Friday evening for an all-night poker game. It was a regular event, but there was one thing different on this particular Friday. It was the new maid's first night. She was from Tupelo, Mississippi, and had never worked for rich folks before, much less seen a high-stakes poker game.

Her eyes bugged out when one player threw a red chip in the middle of the table and said, "I open for one hundred dollars." She dropped the tray with a crash when another threw in a blue chip and said, "I'll raise you five hundred dollars." But the climax came when a third player produced a single yellow chip and declared, "Let's make it one thousand dollars and keep out the riff-raff."

After the last guest had gone, the maid tiptoed into the game room, stole all the chips, and took the next bus back to Tupelo.

Immediately following the invention of money was the invention of poor people. Money has been changing hands for at least twenty-five hundred years. At first, it was in the form of coins. Although there were probably coins of some type used earlier in the Indus Valley and in China, Herodotus places the invention of precious-metal coins in Asia Minor. He reported that all (all?) of the young women of Lydia prostituted themselves in order to procure their marriage portion. They are the first people on record who coined gold and silver into money and traded in retail.

Herodotus also told the story (related in Chapter Three) of Khufu's daughter's using the same method of "retail" to acquire her memorial pyramid, which would place the use of coinage some two thousand years earlier — if you can count stone blocks as coins, and well you might, for money has been represented throughout early history by stones, shells, rags, chunks of metal, cattle, tobacco and whiskey.

Coins were more popular than other forms of money, but you could carry only so many and the quality had to be regulated, as unscrupulous people would "sweat," or clip off, some of the precious metal and accumulate the scraps to make more coins. This problem was solved by the formation of banks, which weighed the coins to insure their value, keeping some of them for their services.

This worked out so well that bank notes — backed by gold and silver, not rocks — were thought up by a Scotsman named John Law. He opened a bank in Paris, and the term "millionaire" was invented when everybody got rich — on paper. Things went well until people began to bring the notes in to claim their silver and gold. According to John Kenneth Galbraith, in *The Age of Uncertainty*, "The Prince deConti sent three wagons to carry back the gold to which his notes entitled him." After this run on the bank, John Law barely escaped Paris with his life, and Galbraith says, "Parisians got what pleasure they could from a song that recommended that the paper be put to the most vulgar possible use."

If coinage was the invention of the Greeks, and if the Scotch, French, Dutch, Italian and English were the originators of banking, credit for paper money in the Western world may be given to the Americans and the Canadians. Galbraith says:

> The birthplace was Massachusetts; the year was 1690. Massachusetts soldiers had just returned from an unsuccessful expedition against Quebec. The loot from the fortress was to have been their pay but there was a miscalculation. Quebec did not fall. Angry soldiers can be a source of unease. So, in the absence of real money — gold or silver — they were given promises of such money instead. These promissory notes then passed from hand to hand as money.

Though this may not be the first use of paper money in the world (the Sung Dynasty, as mentioned earlier, had it four or five hundred years before), the point is that when paper representation of money did arrive, it made possible the use of fantasy in the world of finance.

There is probably not more than two or three thousand dollars in actual cash in circulation today. All the rest of the money you hear about doesn't exist. It is conversation money. When you hear of a transaction involving $50,000,000 it means that one firm wrote $50,000,000 on a piece of paper and gave it to another firm, and the other firm took it home and said, "Look, Momma, I got $50,000,000!" But when Momma asked for a dollar and a quarter to pay the paperboy, the answer probably was that the firm didn't have more than seventy cents in cash.

> *There are some who, in a fifty-fifty proposition, insist on getting the hyphen.*
> — Dr. Laurence J. Peter

A person who deprives himself of everyday pleasures in order to hoard money is called a miser. A person who lives pleasurably within his income is called a magician. There is another type who wants the hoarded money *and* the pleasures of life, and this person shall be called greedy.

Greed is what keeps swindlers in business. "There's one born every minute" and "Never give one an even break" are standard references to suckers. Many fortunes have been made by swindlers using Ponzi schemes or investments in land, oil wells, diamonds, commodities, and other "get-rich-quick" scams.

During the Great Telephone Sales Land Rush of the late 1960s and early 70s, one telephone salesman used to answer the question asked by anxious buyers on the other end of the phone: "Can I come down to see the property?" with "I don't know — can you swim?" And the prospect still bought, after a few uncomfortable chuckles over the apparent joke. Why? Because of greed. They were told by the boys in the boiler-rooms that a big, well-known corporation just bought thousands of acres "right across the road" from the property they were being given an option to buy. This, they were told, would increase the value of their property tenfold. The fact was, the big, well-known corporation — as was discovered when the scam was exposed — actually owned the property that was being sold, and the only thing across the road was P.T. Barnum's ghost — in a boat.

It is hard to tell the difference between greed for money and greed for power. The remark "Money is power" is a conundrum. George G. Kirstein, in *The Rich: Are They Different?*, makes the following observation:

> Because of its nebulous qualities power can be perceived more easily than it can be defined, and this becomes easily apparent when we contrast the rich man's ability to defend his self-interest with the poor man's vulnerability. The poor man's home can be

taken away from him, and frequently is, by some depersonalized combination of forces identifiable to him only as "they." [There They are again!]

His job can disappear not through any fault of his own but because "they" don't need him anymore. The poor have become accustomed to being shoved around; sometimes they almost seem to expect it. "They" — that anonymous conspiracy of the faceless — do the shoving, and resistance, though tempting, is futile. If "they" start shoving the rich around, "they" are quickly identified and promptly encounter resistance.

While Kirstein is correct in his observation, there are occasional examples of someone's getting "fed up" with Them and doing something about it besides taking names. One man, wanting to borrow some money to make a six-month tour of Europe, went to a bank where he had been doing business for years. The bank refused the loan. The man went to another bank and obtained the loan without any difficulty. Then he went to a fish market, bought a five-pound fish, had it wrapped, and put it in his safe-deposit box at the first bank before he joyfully left town for six months.

When this kind of thing happens on a large scale — and not necessarily with fish as the weapon — it is called rebellion. As Kirstein points out, "Being highly educated, the rich are quite aware of history's lessons and are keenly sensitive to social unrest which they know threatens their position more seriously than does reform." To combat this threat, *obliviosus* invented politics.

They say it's the responsibility of the media to look at government — especially at the President — with a

*microscope. I don't argue with that, but when they use
a proctoscope, it's going too far.*
— Richard M. Nixon

There is nothing wrong with a political joke, as long as he isn't elected. As They say, all's fair in love and war — and political persiflage. During a campaign in an illiterate area of the backwoods, one candidate was sharing shouted confidences about his opponent: "Are you good folks aware that my opponent is a known *extrovert*? He has a sister who went to New York City and wasn't there a month before she fell in with a crowd of *thespians*. Furthermore, my opponent spends most of his spare time with *enigmas* and, worst of all, before he was married, he habitually practiced *mastication*." Needless to say, his opponent lost the election.

If it weren't for government, we wouldn't have politicians. In *The Conquest of Civilization*, Breasted traces the beginnings of government back to the Stone Age: "It required power over men and successful management of them to move great blocks of stone for building the chieftain's tomb." Stonehenge is thought to be a chieftain's burial site, and "Hail to the Chief" is a favorite tune of government, even today.

In ancient Egypt, two thousand years before they began stacking stones into pyramids, the Egyptians dug irrigation trenches and canals. According to Breasted:

> Such work on the canals required a leader who was more than a mere fighter, and eventually some intelligent and courageous man seized control in each group of Delta villages, probably over seven thousand years ago. The leader of one of these groups of Delta villages would in time become a local chieftain who

controlled the irrigation works in a large district.

To him the people of the district were obliged to carry every season a share of the grain or flax which they gathered from their fields. If they did not do so, the supply of water in the irrigation trenches for their fields would be stopped by the chieftain, and they would receive an unpleasant visit from him or his men, demanding instant payment. These were the earliest taxes, and the chieftain's control of the canals and collection of such taxes formed the earliest government.

In ancient Greece, a lien or mortgage on a landowner's property was represented by a stone placed on it. Many fields were dotted with stones. If that method were used today, some properties would look like they had been subjected to a major landslide.

Throughout the ages, the methods of government have continued to advance. According to Dr. Laurence J. Peter, "We have two forms of government today: the long form and the short form." Tax collecting and the distribution by the government of more money than is taken in has become a science. In order to simplify things for both you and the government, the short form *à la coup de grace* is presently being drafted: (A) What is your name? (B) How much did you make? (C) Send (B).

> *Men are so simple, and so subject to present necessities, that he who seeks to deceive will always find someone who will allow himself to be deceived.*
> — Niccolò Machiavelli

Two men were discussing the high rate of taxes and the government's waste of money. Just then a school bus passed by.

"See what I mean," exclaimed one. "When I was a boy we walked three miles to school and three miles back home each day. Now we spend $45,000 for a bus to pick up the children so they don't have to walk. Then we spend $250,000 for a gymnasium so they can get exercise."

In *Fat City: How Washington Wastes Your Taxes*, Donald Lambro takes a proctoscopic look at one hundred nonessential federal programs. Published in 1980, some of the programs may have been discontinued by now; if so, it is a certainty that they have been replaced by others just as awe-inspiring. Following are a few select illustrations of how government spends the tax money scraped from the paychecks of *obliviosus* (the examples, from Lambro's book, are not jokes — or if they are, you know who they're on):

National Endowment For The Arts and National Endowment For The Humanities
(Combined budget: $300 million)
— $10,000 for a sixty-minute documentary film about the Pachuco Zootsuiters (a group of Chicano youths in the 1940s);
— $6000 to a Pittsburgh artist who filmed crepe paper and burning gases being dropped out of two small airplanes over the Caribbean resort island of St. Maarten, where the artist and her husband, who was the cameraman, stayed for one week during one of the worst winters to hit the United States.

Federal Trade Commission
(Budget: $65 million)
— $52,700 for the purchase and mailing of cigarettes used for testing advertising practices;

154

— $41,900 for a survey on the effectiveness of corrective advertising for Listerine;

— $20,900 to conduct a survey on the genericness of the trademark Formica in the public's mind.

Economic Research Service
(Budget: $30 million)
Various studies and reports, such as:
— Computer Decision-Making Seen as an Aid to Baking;
— The Changing Patterns of Eating Out;
— Mobile Home Residents in New Hampshire;
— Consumers' Preferences for Fresh Tomatoes.

Those are just a sampling of the billions of dollars a year spent on *ad hoc* programs that go on *ad infinitum* to become *ad nauseam*. When that point is reached, the National Science Foundation Low Priority Research Program, which cost $90,000, may be applied: the study of facial muscle activity accompanying low-intensity emotional states.

In the face of these taxing programs, if a grimace doesn't help, you may decide to give up and go to a movie. Why not see one of the Navy's $64,000 film series: *How to Succeed With Brunettes*, the subject of which is etiquette for officers, or *Blondes Prefer Gentlemen*, a Navy epic that demonstrates how to maneuver suavely through a dinner party.

* * *

A man had barely paid off the mortgage on his house when he mortgaged it again to buy a car. Then he sought out a loan company to try to borrow money on the car so he could build a garage.

"If we make you the loan," asked the man at the finance company, "how will you buy gas for the car?"

"It seems to me," the man replied in an injured tone, "that a fellow who owns his own house, car and garage should be able to get credit for gas."

— 14 —

The Sahara Forest and The Grand Canyon Toxic Waste Dump

You can't make it. You can't buy it. And when it's gone, it's gone forever.

— Chief Buffalo Tiger

The line of men moved slowly toward the table where a foreman was hiring workers for a new logging company. One by one, the huge men shuffled up to the table, answered a couple of questions, and signed their names.

The foreman looked up to see a small, frail man standing before him. The foreman smiled at the man, who was dwarfed by the giants standing behind him in line. The tiny, middle-aged man couldn't have weighed more than ninety pounds, soaking wet.

Still smiling, the foreman decided to let the man down gently. "Sir, do you have any experience in lumberjacking?" he asked.

"Yes," the little man replied. "I worked for many years in the Sahara Forest."

The foreman looked around at some of the big men, who were also smiling. "Sahara Forest?" he inquired. "You mean the Sahara Desert, don't you?"

The little man shrugged his shoulders and said, "Sure, *now!*"

Fossil remains and cave paintings on the Tassili plateau are evidence that luxuriant vegetation once covered the Sahara. From satellites using infrared photography, traces of huge river systems etched into this now dry and barren world are visible.

There is a pattern of sorts in the history of natural resources. Nature creates a variety of environments, some of which contain edible plants. Animals come to eat all the plants. Then man comes in to eat all the animals. When nothing is left but the desolate land, man begins to destroy that. According to Carlton S. Coon in *The Races of Europe*: "To a cosmic geographer with a purely objective interest in man, our species would appear as no more than a highly organized form of skin cancer which is destroying the earth's surface with increasing rapidity."

The American Indians had the land for over ten thousand years. During that time, they kept it in pretty much its original condition. In their three hundred years of control, the more recent inhabitants of that land have gouged, stripped, bulldozed, paved, smoked, sprayed and fertilized the environment to the point where, if a buffalo showed up today, it would probably become crazed by the scent of brown air and run into the path of a speeding automobile.

But the American Indians are descendants of *obliviosus*, too. When their forerunners got to South America about ten thousand years ago, they set up housekeeping. Eventually, they became known as Mayans, and they invented a kind of agriculture known as *milpa*, or "slash and burn." According to C.W. Ceram in *Gods, Graves and Scholars* it worked this way:

> The jungle trees and bush were cut down, allowed to dry out, then burned shortly before the onset of the rainy season. The corn was planted with the use of pointed planting sticks, several seeds being dropped in each hole. After the fields were worn out, the farmer moved to another clearing.
>
> The available land supply simply became exhausted. A wide belt of burned and worn-out steppe appeared between the farm land and the cities [until]

the cities were completely surrounded and ultimately linked together by areas of dry, grassy steppe.

Modern science has developed newer and faster ways of defoliating and sterilizing the land, and *obliviosus* is now working on ways to apply the "slash and burn" method to cities, ultimately leaving civilization to lay fallow.

> *We've got to pause and ask ourselves: How much clean air do we need?*
>
> — Lee Iacocca

"What is all this uproar," the scientists say, "about polluting the environment?" They claim that there was nothing more toxic a hundred years ago than when three million horses deposited twenty to twenty-five pounds of manure apiece, per day, on the streets of urban America.

Well, a lot of things can cause air pollution, some obvious, some not so obvious. For example, methane (as in swamp gas) has a greenhouse effect on the atmosphere. Methane is, among other things, a byproduct of digesting cellulose. Cows eat a lot of grass, thereby digesting a lot of cellulose. Science has noted that cows break wind every thirty or forty seconds. (Those scientists have to be everywhere!) Since there are seventeen times as many cows as humans on the planet and since there are a little over five billion people, that figures out to about 170 gigapoops per minute! And our government is making a big stink about cigarette smoke.

In the production of materials and the harnessing of energy, there is a byproduct called waste. *Obliviosus* has developed an uncreative method of handling waste matter: bury it. John G.

Mitchell, in his book *Losing Ground*, reports a conversation with a gas and electric company engineer:

> "And what will they do with all the spoil from the excavations?"
> "Dump it," said the engineer. "If we get the permit, mostly in Lost Canyon."
> "Perfect," I said. "When the canyon is all filled up, you won't even have to change its name."

A 1983 newspaper item reported a proposal to utilize Bryce Canyon in Utah as a toxic waste dump. The experience of smaller efforts like this is invaluable. When Bryce fills up, they can move on down to the Grand Canyon and start on that. It might be a good idea, after all. At the time of the Bryce Canyon item, there were over fourteen thousand potentially hazardous toxic chemical dump sites spread throughout America. If they use the Grand Canyon, the rest of the country could be cleaned up, and everyone would just stay away from Arizona.

Arizona already has some experience as a dumping ground. In 1986, it was discovered that in 1982 a break in an underground pipeline pumped over one hundred thousand gallons of jet fuel into a citrus orchard near Yuma. The state's Department of Health Services had an immediate solution — they dumped seventeen tons of steer manure on the fuel spill to sop it up. Confronted with this story in 1986, a DHS official put his hands over his face and said: "Oh, no! Not the bull ＿＿＿＿ theory!"

> *When you get there there isn't any there there.*
> — Gertrude Stein

U.S. Planned To Use A-Bombs
To Clear Way For Interstate

Riverside — Federal officials proposed using twenty-two atomic bombs to vaporize a huge chunk of mountain in 1964 to straighten the path of Interstate 40 through the Mojave Desert, newly released government documents say. The plan, later scuttled for budgetary reasons, was to use the bombs, equivalent to 1.73 million tons of TNT, to clear sixty-eight million tons of the Bristol Mountains and save fifteen miles of highway construction, the documents indicate.

— Newspaper item

Surely *obliviosus* is not so oblivious, or stupid, as to do something like use nuclear bombs to clear highway right-of-ways? Not to worry, the Atomic Energy Commission performed a technical study at the time of the above proposal and "largely dismissed," according to the article, "radiation danger in connection with the plan."

The AEC should know about radiation danger, having had so much experience with it. Although (to date) there has never been an accidental detonation of a U.S. nuclear weapon, there have been a few close calls. Following is a sampling of accidents reported in the 1983 *Book of Lists #3*:

Goldsboro, N.C., Jan. 24, 1961

A B-52 fell apart in midair, killing three out of eight crew members and releasing two twenty-four-megaton nuclear bombs. (All of the bombs dropped on Germany and Japan during W.W. II totaled 2.2 megatons.) One bomb parachuted to the ground and was recovered, but the other fell free and landed in waterlogged farmland, never to be found. When the recovered bomb was studied, it was discovered that five of its six safety devices had failed.

Damascus, Ark., Sept. 19, 1980

An Air Force repairman doing routine maintenance in a Titan II ICBM silo dropped a wrench socket, which rolled off a work platform and fell to the bottom of the silo. The socket struck the missile, causing a leak from a pressurized fuel tank. The missile complex and surrounding area were evacuated. Eight and a half hours later, fuel vapors ignited, causing an explosion which killed an Air Force specialist and injured twenty-one others. The explosion also blew off the 740-ton reinforced concrete-and-steel silo door and catapulted the nuclear warhead six hundred feet into the air. The silo has since been filled with gravel, and operations have been transferred to a similar installation at Rock, Kansas [with, we hope, an airman at the bottom of the silo with a wrench-socket catcher's mitt].

Scotland, Nov. 2, 1981

Scotland was almost obliterated when a fully armed Poseidon missile was accidentally dropped seventeen feet from a crane during a transfer operation between a U.S. submarine and its mother ship.

These are just a few examples; there are many others. Is it unfair and biased doomsaying to select a few near-disasters and blow them (excuse the expression) out of proportion? No, it is just an interesting pastime, a part of observing *obliviosus* as he merrily wends his way to catastrophe. After all, we have been reassured by a committee of scientists (Doc, Sneezy, Dopey . . .)

that there is no danger.

The fact that forty percent of the nuclear submarines of the United States, representing over one hundred floating nuclear reactors, are based near the heavily-populated San Francisco bay area and at the juncture of two major earthquake faults, shouldn't bother us in the least.

* * *

The three-star general fed his problem into the gigantic Pentagon computer: should he move a large nuclear weapon storage facility to the West Coast or to the East Coast?

In a matter of seconds, the computer ejected its answer on a small, white card: "Yes."

Perturbed, the general quickly fed another question into the machine: "Yes, what?"

The computer ejected a second card: "Yes, SIR!"

– 15 –

Slouching Towards Armageddon

Do not needlessly endanger your lives until I give you the signal.
— Dwight D. Eisenhower

At the beginning of World War II, the officer in charge of a British post deep in the heart of Africa received a wireless message from his superior officer: "War declared. Arrest all enemy aliens in your district."

In about four hours, a wire was sent from the post to command headquarters: "Have arrested seven Germans, three Belgians, two Frenchmen, two Italians, an Austrian, and an American. Please say whom we are at war with."

Scholars say that from 1469 B.C. to A.D. 1861, a period of 3,330 years, there were 227 years of peace and 3,103 years of war. For the past hundred years or so, not only have they lost count, but no one can name the 227 years that organized warfare was not in progress in one part of the world or another.

According to various interpretations of the Bible, Armageddon, the final conclusive battle between the forces of good and evil, is supposed to take place near Megiddo, on the Plain of Jezreel in Palestine. In 1469 B.C., the first battle described in recorded history took place at Megiddo.

Before one hearkens to the whispers of coincidence, one would do well to remember that armed conflict goes back to Cain and Abel. Or, if one prefers a more scientific reference, to Neolithic man, whose skeletons have been unearthed with flint arrowheads sticking in bones and eyeholes. One Neolithic skeleton, a man of huge size, was discovered with one arm almost severed from the shoulder by a stone ax, a fragment of which was still imbedded in the arm bone.

Throughout history, *obliviosus* has taken up arms and done battle over the two main sources of power: land and gold. Sometimes the two are confused. The atrocities committed by Columbus and his followers in the name of discovery were actually the means of a ruthless search for gold. On the other hand, war may result from a defense of the homeland, which implies an attacker of the homeland. The grass is always greener on the other side of the Euphrates. Around 2300 B.C., Sargon conquered the Sumerians in the fertile valley of the two rivers. Actually, one of the reasons he wanted the land was because it was necessary to protect the silver trade route.

> *By Abraham! noble Sir, those greaves become your legs!*
> *Pull them in a bit at the ankles, Isaac!*
> — Edward Lester Arnold,
> *The Wonderful Adventures of Phra the Phoenician*

Ah, the glamour of war: the uniforms with shiny buttons, the rattle of sabers, the thundering hoofbeats of the cavalry arriving just in time, etc., including a few casualties. But, then, what are a few casualties when the survivors can bask in the glory of victory?

Obliviosus seems to like warfare so much, if it were possible to resurrect the hundreds of millions who have died as a result of warfare (organized, not including domestic squabbles, neighborhood frays, Saturday night altercations and other unorganized battles), they would probably choose up sides and start all over, if someone could convince them that this time, they would be the victor.

Often, however, it is difficult to tell just who is victorious. In *The Living Past*, Lissner tells of Hannibal's fate:

> In fifteen years in Italy, Hannibal had not lost a single battle. On one occasion he had come within three miles of Rome. Nothing but weeds grew in the fields of Italy. Hundreds of towns lay in ruins. The bones of Carthaginian soldiers and pack animals bleached on the Alpine passes. Hundreds of thousands of Romans and Roman allies had been killed. All this Hannibal had achieved. He was one of the greatest military geniuses of the ancient world, perhaps second only to Alexander the Great. And it had all been in vain.

The reason it had been in vain was that while Hannibal was laying waste to Italy, the Romans conquered Carthage, and Hannibal had no home to which to return. At fifty years of age, he was sent into exile in the East.

> *I do like to see the arms and legs fly.*
> — George S. Patton III

The main purpose of a weapon is lethality, and *obliviosus* has been continually improving the lethality of weapons throughout history. Weapons fall into two major categories: shock and missile. Some are a combination of both. The earliest weapons were sticks and stones. The sticks could be used as clubs, but, if they were sharpened and thrown or shot, they became missiles. The stones could also be used as striking objects but were more effective when hurled from slings. Early armies were made up of throwers, shooters, stabbers, clubbers and slingers. Warfare at the time must have seemed a little hectic. No wonder the word *panic* — after the mischievous Greek god Pan — was coined at the battle of Marathon.

Occasionally, a weapon appears to be out of chronological sequence. For example, one would think that Pyrrhus (c. 280 B.C.), the Greek who was ranked with Alexander and Hannibal as one of the greatest warriors of all time and who commanded an army of well-trained Greek infantry, the world's best cavalry of Thessalian horsemen, and a formidable herd of fighting elephants, would have been done in only by a greater foe with a secret weapon unavailable to Pyrrhus. In a way, that is what happened. He was slain at Argos by a woman who snatched a tile from a housetop and hurled it at his head as he rode into town.

In his efforts to improve the lethality of weapons, *obliviosus* invented gunpowder, bullets, shells, bombs, guided missiles and nuclear explosions. In *The Evolution of Weapons and Warfare*, Colonel (Ret.) T. N. Dupuy offers a Theoretical Lethality Index (TLI), which is a table representing a number of factors, including the number of potential targets per strike. The TLI of a sword is listed at 23. The TLI of a World War II machine gun is 4,973. The TLI of a World War II medium tank is 575,000. The (1980) TLI of a one-megaton nuclear airburst is 695,385,000.

Military intelligence is a contradiction in terms.
— Groucho Marx

A child was hearing about wars and asked his father how they got started.

"Suppose America quarreled with England . . ." the father started to say, when he was interrupted by the mother.

"But England and America aren't quarreling," the mother said.

Father: "I know, but this is only an example."

Mother: "But you are misleading the child."

Father: "No, I'm not."

Mother: "Yes, you are!"

Father: "I tell you I'm not! And if you don't quit interrupting . . ."

Child: "Never mind, Dad. I think I understand now."

There is more to the story of warfare than weapons. Tactics have been, in many cases, more important than the weaponry involved and have been in evidence ever since Thutmosis III flanked the Palestinians at Megiddo in 1469 B.C. *Obliviosus* has gone on from there to develop the ultimate aid to tactical warfare: the computer.

One of the most recent examples is "Janus." Named for the two-faced Roman god, the world's most powerful computerized combat simulator is used by the Defense Department and the U.S. Army War College. The computer can display in full topographical detail any fifteen-square-mile area of the earth.

According to articles in several magazines, the computer has been equipped with colorful detail. As the action mounts, "land mines explode in flashes of white . . . artillery fire slashes across the screen like a laser sword . . . towns are reduced to rubble . . . forests erupt in flames." As one Lieutenant Colonel said, "You get a real feeling for the dynamics and pressures of combat." Not as much as a dirk in the groin, Colonel, but at least you learn something.

The articles relate the story of one officer who let his position deteriorate beyond recovery. He picked the largest weapon in his megaton arsenal and dropped it where he guessed the Red Army had massed. The bomb detonated in a flash of orange, and a growing white circle indicated the destruction of his opponent's forces. But he had chosen a weapon so powerful that it also wiped out his own troops. His only comment, according to the articles, was a subdued "Holy smoke."

Computer warfare is an ambivalence in terms. A computer can be used to simulate or to assist in warfare, or warfare may be used against computers. Many strategists (and some terrorists) have concluded that, if computers can be disabled or caused to malfunction, an advantage would be gained in the event of war.

One method of doing this is known as EMP, or the creation of electromagnetic pulses by exploding a nuclear device in the upper atmosphere, sending the pulses throughout the entire enemy country, which would render inoperative any electronic device, resulting in a complete breakdown of communications.

Another method of warfare against computers involves actually using them, but in a perverse way to create chaos. In "Computer War," a special report in *Science Digest*, Richard Conniff said that electronic terrorism might be used to cause commercial disaster by having the computers send parts needed in Detroit on Tuesday to Los Angeles on Wednesday instead. One of the most terrifying ideas cited by Conniff in the article was the destruction of computers that handle unemployment and welfare checks. Imagine telling the guys on the street corner in Miami — on a hot summer day — that the computer's down.

A single death is a tragedy, a million deaths is a statistic.

— Joseph Stalin

From the American Revolution through Vietnam, approximately 1,150,000 Americans have died in wars. The last widow of the American Revolution, Catherine S. Damon, died in 1906. The last widow of the War of 1812, Carolina King, died in 1936. The last widow of the Mexican War, Lena James Theobald, died in 1963. There have been more widows of war created in the last forty-five years than there were in the first 165 years.

Apparently without realizing it, *obliviosus* now has at his disposal the means to solve the fatality problem connected with warfare. H.G. Wells, in 1913, published a book called *Little Wars*. It was a compendium of miniature wargames, using plastic soldiers, cardboard buildings, and guns that fired little wooden pellets. As Wells says about the miniature wargame:

> How much better is this amiable miniature than the Real Thing! Here is the premeditation, the thrill, the strain of accumulating victory or disaster — and no smashed or sanguinary bodies, no shattered fine buildings nor devastated countrysides, no petty cruelties, none of that awful universal boredom and embitterment that we who are old enough to remember a real modern war know to be the reality of belligerence.

Evidently, the book didn't sell well or the idea didn't take, for the next year was 1914, the beginning of World War I, which, Isaac Asimov says in his foreword to the 1970 reprint of Wells' book, was a war of "incredible stupidity on the part of the generals."

In *From the Jaws of Victory*, by Charles Fair, many wars are seen to be "mostly left to bad generals and clumsy-minded statesmen." Fair relates the story of a Union soldier in the War Between the States who had spent the night before fraternizing with Confederate pickets across the Rappahannock and then wrote home to his wife: "If the war had been left to us, we would have settled it in fifteen minutes."

If *obliviosus* could merge the idea of miniature wargames with the marvels of computer technology, actual warfare could be eliminated. A battle could be staged between countries on linked computers — possibly every weekend, like the old Friday Night Fights — with the winner receiving predetermined amounts of land and gold. The people of the losing nations would wear black armbands for three days to symbolize defeat, and the generals who operated the losing computer programs would be either flogged with nettles or tickled mercilessly in order to satisfy the need for aggression.

> *We live in a Newtonian world of Einsteinian physics ruled by Frankensteinian logic.*
> — David Russell

A jug of wine, a loaf of bread . . . etc. In the event of a surprise nuclear attack, there would hardly be time to grab a can of beer and a small order of fries. A 1983 newspaper item reported that there was concern as to whether a helicopter would have time to get from the White House to Andrews Air Force Base — at a speed of 625 miles per hour — in the event of a surprise nuclear attack on the capital. Yet the Federal Emergency Management Agency (FEMA) has devised very detailed plans for evacuation in the event of a nuclear attack. An evacuation scenario might go something like this:

There would be a warning. In the case of land-based missiles, thirty minutes; submarine-launched, fifteen minutes; subs off the

U.S. coast, eight to twelve minutes. OK, here they come! Within six miles of the epicenter of a one-megaton blast, the effect is similar to dropping the family dictionary on your pet turtle, so you must get to a point at least six miles from the epicenter — assuming you know which intersection in your city will be the epicenter — for a fifty-fifty chance of survival. You would have a 90 percent chance twelve miles away.

FEMA figures an evacuation rate of one thousand vehicles per lane, per hour. That averages out to about three miles per hour, bumper-to-bumper, with an ETA at the fifty-fifty chance point of two hours, and an ETA of four hours at the 90 percent point, unless somebody pulls out to pass. Bear in mind that in order for evacuation to work, it must be orderly . . . five thousand people were trampled to death at Czar Nicholas II's coronation ceremony in the stampede for free beer.

Assuming a maximum of eight lanes per road (all outgoing, of course), times the four compass points (and subtracting new roads being instantly invented), that comes to thirty-two lanes or thirty-two thousand vehicles per hour, casually driving out of town at three miles per hour under the threat of imminent nuclear attack.

If each vehicle has four occupants (perhaps more, since certainly everyone will pick up hitchhikers — at three miles per hour, how can you prevent it?), that comes to about 128,000 evacuees per hour. At that rate, New York City should be clear in three days. Yazoo City, Mississippi, with about twelve thousand population — if it had thirty-two lanes outgoing — could make it in six minutes.

Aside from evacuation, is the government doing any other preparatory planning for the event of nuclear attack? You bet your neutrons! Everyone, of course, made fun of the remark made by Thomas K. Jones, President Reagan's Deputy Under-Secretary of Defense: "Dig a hole, cover it with a couple of doors, and then throw three feet of dirt on top. Everyone's going to make it if there are enough shovels to go around."

This idea was ridiculed by everyone exposed to it, in and out of the federal bureaucracy. To show that they are indeed sober and responsible representatives of the people they serve, the various agencies of the government quickly attempted to close the credibility gap with the following survival plans:

— The Department of Agriculture has a food-rationing system to distribute, among other items, six eggs and four pounds of cereal each week to every surviving American. Delivery should be easy: just dig up three feet of dirt and knock on the door.

— The U.S. Postal Service will issue postage-free "emergency-change-of-address cards." A spokesman says, "Those that are left will get their mail." (From whom?) This branch of the government also has stocked food and medical supplies for their workers. Since most main branches, where the food is stored, are located downtown, and since metal melts within a 3.5-mile-radius of the epicenter, their pork and beans will be cooked for them.

— The Internal Revenue Service, assuming that computerized tax records would probably be destroyed, has proposed a sales tax to support the government until the tax system can be restored.

— The Department of Housing and Urban Development has a procedure for requisitioning houses "whose owners have disappeared."

— FEMA has devised a plan for Washington, D.C., in which the evacuation of citizens calls for people driving cars with odd-numbered plates to wait for those with even-numbered plates to leave the city first, which accounts for the personalized license plates spelling out TWO, FOUR, SIX, etc.

The only proper response to the victims of serious burns, broken bones, crush injuries and radiation who might have been unlucky enough to survive a nuclear attack is mercy killing, according to a British doctor critical of the government's civil-defense plans. The physician prescribed the following treatment in case of nuclear war: "As no drugs will have been stockpiled for the population at large, it would appear that the best thing that could be done for them would be to hit them over the head with a large stone."

This is the first age that's paid much attention to the future, which is a little ironic since we may not have one.
— Arthur C. Clarke

In the *New York Times Book Review* of April 8, 1984, Michael Howard, in a review entitled "Making the World Safe for Conventional War," made the following comment:

Is this yet another of those works, of which Jonathan Schell's was the most publicized and Lewis Thomas's *Late Night Thoughts* the most recent example, that explain our predicament to us in beautiful prose, tell us how *stupid* we all are and exhort us to repent without being very specific as to what we should actually *do* about it?

Those books, and others like them (not to mention you-know-which), are probably hoping to make *obliviosus* at least aware of the present situation. As for solutions, they have ranged from the sublime to the ridiculous, and it is difficult to tell which is which — from complete disarmament of all nations (we can't even disarm the NRA) to a trampoline-type device that would kick invading ICBM's back to where they came from. One writer suggested that the United States should project a giant hologram of Tijuana into our atmosphere to confuse the Russian rockets.

The reason no one has come up with a viable answer to what we should actually do about the threat of nuclear destruction is that no one really believes it will happen. After all, we are sitting safe and sound on Edgar's lap, aren't we? Surely he wouldn't make such a stupid mistake as to pull the wrong string . . . would he?

> *HELP!*
> — Increasingly common expression

A man once met a disturbed young lady who complained that she could not live on an island. She told him she had a deep-seated fear of islands. "They give me claustrophobia," she said.

The man, a little older and wiser, knew from his experience that the best way to calm a phobia-ridden friend is to trot out phobias of your own. He told the girl, "I know exactly how you feel. I have somewhat the same problem."

"You get uneasy on islands, too?" she asked eagerly.

"Not islands, exactly," the man admitted gravely. "I'm uneasy on continents."

Maybe the end will not come with a bang, but with a whimper. In the science fiction novel, *The Stars In Shroud*, Gregory Benford devised an interesting psychological weapon by which the alien Quarn use direct sensory input to release primeval human fears of being crowded. The entire human population is destroyed by mass psychosis as people desperately avoid one another and crawl into holes in the ground.

If this happened, not remembering that he had been there before, man would return to the cave to cower by the fire and draw pictures on the walls of how it once was. And to carve images and make tools. And, one day, not thinking, to pick up a rock to throw at someone who was bothering him.

* * *

Teenagers Find Brain At Bus Stop

Gainesville [Florida] — Two teenage boys found a human brain on the ground at their school bus stop, but officials said no foul play was suspected. "I thought somebody had been killed and the brain had been left behind," said one of the two fourteen-year-old boys who discovered the brain Friday.

The chief medical examiner said officials have been unable to determine who removed the brain, where it came from or how it ended up on a city street.

— News item April 28, 1986

We know, doctor. We know.

Apology:
What You Thought I Said Was Not What I Think I Meant

A footnote is like running downstairs to answer the doorbell during the first night of marriage.
— John Barrymore

Horace Greeley, who always insisted that the word "news" was plural, once wired a reporter: "Are there any news?" The reply came back by return wire: "Not a new."

The way mankind has continually repeated its follies throughout history lends credence to the adage: no new is good new. And so it goes with the history of the creature we have called *Homo obliviosus*. Examples of strange behavior abound, and the ones used here are but one perspective on the history of mankind, offered in the same spirit as the poor girl in an Applachian school who was made to write and sign a statement before the final exam: "I ain't received no help, and God knows I couldn't have gave any."

Anyone who writes of history must deal with bits of information passed on in many forms, most of which are not complete, and all of which are colored by interpretation and even, in many cases, invention. "Facts" are generally recognized by corroboration, but many reports are singular and, therefore, unsubstantiated. Every quotation, statement, or opinion that could be attributed, has been attributed — hopefully to the right person. (Attributions, in literature, seem to drift somehow.) Anything that is not attributed can be blamed on the author who is, after all, a member of the *Homo obliviosus* species.

Credits have been given in the body of the work. Footnotes or chapter notes have not been used because they generally serve two main purposes, both of which are at odds with the reader's interest: first, explanation, and second, citation. With little effort, the citations are given and the explanations are made in the flow of the telling, and not repeated in another place. When footnotes begin to take up more space on the page than the story itself (one example at hand has one inch of story and five inches of footnote on the same page), the reader feels like he's reading two books simultaneously. If the footnotes are that interesting, perhaps the author should have used them to compose another book — probably more interesting than the one footnoted.

Here lies King Jake
He was killed by a snake.
(His name was not Jake but El Cid,
But El Cid would not rhyme with snake, and Jake did.)
— BL

As to names and spelling, we have taken a position alongside T. E. Lawrence, who is reported in the preface to *The Seven Pillars of Wisdom* to have said: "Arabic names [nor some used here] won't go into English exactly, for their consonants are not the same as ours, and their vowels, like ours, vary from district to district. There are some 'scientific systems' of transliteration, helpful to people who know enough Arabic not to need helping, but a washout for the world. I spell my names anyhow, to show what rot the systems are."

The spellings and names used throughout this book are either the most commonly used, or the ones given in the original sources. Most people feel, like Humpty-Dumpty, "When *I* use a word, it means just what I choose it to mean — neither more nor less." If you saw SLMN written, and you had to add the vowels (omitted in the original alphabets), would you make it Solomon? Suliman? Saal-Amen? Sal Mineo? As long as whatever word chosen refers to the same thing, idea or person and is generally recognizable, it will work for communication. What the Greeks called Hecatombean, we call July, but that doesn't make it any cooler.

> *In China, the land of the tong,*
> *A post-dinner speaker is wrong*
> *If all he can say is*
> *I won't leave the dais*
> *Until I have been On Too Long.*
> — BL

Realizing that lectures are like pigeons: you like them as long as they're not over your head, I have tried to maintain a balance between information and entertainment in this book. I hope it worked, because sometimes you mean well but the results may not be quite what you expected. Kind of like the farmer whose cow took sick. He went to the vet for advice, and the vet told him that all he needed to do was administer a little mineral oil through a funnel into the cow's south end.

Well, the farmer looked around the house but could find no mineral oil. He did find a gallon can of jalapeños in the kitchen, and it said "Packed in Oil" on the label, so he figured that would do. He drained off the oil into a jar and headed out to the barn.

The cow watched in a sickly, walleyed way as the farmer hunted for a funnel. There was none, but he did spot an old, rusted French horn hanging on a nail. Brushing away the cobwebs and wiping off the rust from the mouthpiece, the farmer decided it would do for a funnel.

As he inserted the French horn, the cow's eyes got a little wallier, but when he poured the jalapeño oil into the bell the cow tightened its grip on the horn, its eyes shut tightly for a couple of seconds, then blinked open in a stare of terror. All in one motion, the cow kicked down the stall, busted a hole in the wall of the barn and took off across the fields — front end bellowing a miserable lament and the rear end blowing harmony on the French horn.

Finally, the poor animal got to the river, jumped in and started swimming upstream against the strong current. It might have ended there, but the bridgekeeper heard it, thought it was a ship coming downstream, and raised the drawbridge.

When the bridgekeeper saw — and heard — a singing cow playing a French horn swimming backwards under the bridge, he decided that this would be a good time to quit drinking and start going back to church.

Acknowledgments

Not inexperienced in misfortune, I have learned to aid the wretched.

— Virgil

I would like to thank the following for their aid, suggestions (even though they may have been ignored) and encouragement (which was always appreciated):

I am especially grateful to Sydney J. Stanley, Senior Librarian of the Mission Hills Branch of the San Diego Public Library. Sydney read the original draft as I was writing it and gave me the support I needed at the most difficult times. Although she cannot be *blamed* for anything in the book, without her help I probably wouldn't have written it. (But she shouldn't be blamed for that either.)

I would also like to thank all of the librarians at the Phoenix Public Library, especially Fern Eckhardt, who went out of her way and beyond the library's facilities to seek out obscure items for me.

Because some things cannot be found out, even in libraries, I must acknowledge the help I received from the personnel of every new and used book store in Phoenix and San Diego, especially Barbara Gelink of the Otento Book Store in San Diego. It's not easy to deal with a guy who comes in and asks for "a little brown book — it's about *this* big — on humor that came out about thirty or forty years ago . . . I forget the name of it."

On a more personal level, I must express my sincere gratitude to my cousin in New Orleans, Edward J. Caamano and his wife, Janice. They helped me through a near-fatal hospital stay in 1974, when I was in a coma for ten days. If it weren't for their support, I might be writing this from the other side — that place where all the publishers are. I owe Eddie and Janice more than this paragraph.

Permissions